Technical Tennis

Racquets, Strings, Balls, Courts, Spin, and Bounce

Rod Cross
Crawford Lindsey

Racquet Tech Publishing
Vista, California, USA

Racquet Tech Publishing
(An imprint of the USRSA)
330 Main St.
Vista, California 92084
www.racquettech.com

Library of Congress Control Number: 2005905393

Cover design and illustrations by Kristine Thom
Inside chapter title photos by Ron Waite, Photosportacular

Printed in the United States of America

ISBN-13: 978-0-97227-593-4
ISBN-10: 0-9722759-3-2

Contents

Contents

Foreword

Several years ago, the two authors of this book and I wrote an encyclopedic tome with the imposing title *The Physics and Technology of Tennis*. Even though thousands of copies of this book have been sold and are still selling, and in spite of the fact that it was a Scientific American Book Club selection, it is not for everyone, and only the most motivated have read it from cover to cover. Who ever thought there was so much science to hitting a fuzzy yellow ball? But there is, and it is all there in its 435, 8.5" x 11" pages, including many hundreds of graphs, charts, diagrams, and formulas. It is a tremendous reference book, textbook, or self-teaching manual, but it is not a casual read.

What is needed now is an up-to-date, reader-friendly book that covers the technical parts of tennis in a far less comprehensive and technical manner. It needs to be written so that a tennis player can pick it up, read it, and understand it. This is that book. It is written for tennis players and tennis fans, not engineers, scientists, or over-motivated super-achievers. It is still meaty and an intellectual adventure, but all the technical language has been translated to people-speak within its human-sized 160 pages.

It addresses questions such as:

- When you want a bit more power in your game, should you go to a heavier racquet or a lighter one?
- What are the advantages of a racquet that has a bigger head?
- What effect does string tension have on your game, and how does it affect power and control?
- What is the difference between gut strings and synthetic strings?
- What is the importance of string thickness?
- What is a "fast" court and what is a "slow" court?
- Should you adjust your equipment to match the court speed?
- When buying a racquet, what features should you look for?
- If you want to put more spin on the ball, what should you do?

In my many years of playing tennis and studying tennis, I have heard a lot of anecdotal answers to these questions. This book gives you the answers that science and technology provide.

HOWARD BRODY
Physics Department
University of Pennsylvania

Preface

Much has already been written about tennis, mostly about how to improve your mental and physical game and about famous players. This book is about neither of these topics. It is about racquets, strings, balls, and courts and how they interact with each other and with players. You can play a very good game of tennis (or golf or baseball) without knowing anything about the equipment you use or about ball trajectories, but being aware of the basics can help you avoid common pitfalls. In fact, it is amazing how many of today's top players appear to be unaware of the basics. Watch them when they change ball direction back over the net. They are very good at returning the ball straight back to their opponent, but as soon as they hit away from their opponent, their error rate increases dramatically. There is a simple reason for this. It is always safer to hit the ball straight back to your opponent because the ball will travel back in that direction no matter how hard you hit it. If you try to change the direction of the ball, then the angle of the ball off the strings depends on how fast the ball is traveling toward you and on how hard you hit it. If you know about this, then you will be less likely to aim precisely for the sideline. Chances are, if you aim for the line, the ball will go out.

If you know how and why you are doing a particular action, it may not directly help the performance of the action, but it will enhance your mindset, which in turn influences the performance. If you know why, for example, that tilting your racquet face forward causes more topspin, then you will be more likely to practice doing it with confidence, without those nagging doubts that it is stupid and your instructor is nuts because you obviously can't hit the ball over the net, with topspin no less, while "aiming" into the ground. If you know how much extra power, spin, or comfort you can or cannot get by changing string tensions or by using bigger racquets, then you will be able to make intelligent equipment decisions and not waste emotional and intellectual energy agonizing over whether your trial-and-error guess of what's best for you is really best. Changing strings, tensions, racquets, and customizing weights and balances then become fun, tactical elements of your tennis game, not spin-the-wheel whims of chance.

Knowing what your equipment can and can't do for you makes a big difference in how you approach the game. Knowing how, when, and why the ball grips the strings and how that affects your shot frees you from chasing solutions to getting "more grip" on the ball that not only don't exist, but would have no effect if they did. Understanding why a ball bounces as it does on a topspin, backspin, or sidespin shot enables you to ready yourself, get in position, and anticipate your return of the shot. It eliminates the frustration of being caught flat-footed and clueless time after time. It enables you to make intelligent corrections in your game.

But most of all, knowing what actually happens during the hit, flight, and bounce of the ball and why it happens is just plain fun. To be able to explain how and why the court, racquet, and air affect the speed, spin, and direction of the ball—the very essence of tennis—and thus why strokes, tactics, and strategy have evolved as they have, is a rush matched only by being able to actually do these things. Knowledge and performance combine to provide a much deeper and enjoyable tennis experience, if not a more successful one as well.

For readers who are interested in the technical and scientific aspects of tennis or are just plain curious or are looking for an extra understanding that will give strokes and shots meaning, this book has been written especially for you. It contains the results of many years of investigation and many experiments designed to extract the secrets of how and why tennis balls, racquets, and strings manage to behave the way they do. We still don't know everything there is to know about the subject, but we know a lot more than we used to know. For example, we know very little about players' perceptions of equipment properties and why they are so often quite different from actual measurements of those properties. Likewise, we don't know why one player has a favorite string or racquet and another will think that particular string or racquet is the worst he or she has ever played with. Not knowing all the answers makes the search an adventure, finding them out is exhilarating, and applying them raises the level of the game.

Many people have contributed to this book in many ways. We thank all of them profusely, especially Howard Brody, Ron Kohn, Paul Metzler, Greg Raven, Kristine Thom, Ron Waite, Nancy Crowley, and our wives Voula and Susan.

Chapter One

Racquets

All racquet performance technologies boil down to two things—altering the stiffness of the frame and stringbed and the amount and distribution of weight. These, in turn, determine the power, control, and feel of a racquet.

INTRODUCTION

Hitting a tennis ball is an epic battle between player, racquet, and ball. The player ultimately wants to be able to swing the racquet as fast as possible and to change its direction in a split second, but he does not want the ball to be able to do the same thing to the racquet. He doesn't want the ball pushing the racquet backwards, twisting it in his hand, or bending it out of shape and direction. But making it more difficult for the ball to move the racquet also makes it more difficult for the player to do so. For the player to achieve the most maneuverability, the racquet has to be light, but to prevent the ball from knocking the racquet all over the place, it has to be heavy. And if the ball is pushing the racquet around, power is lost. So, the player also wants the racquet to be heavy to get the most power. But if it is too heavy, he can't swing as fast, and he loses power. What a problem!

CHOOSING A RACQUET—THE BASICS

Given these problems, how does one choose a racquet? First we will start with some general common-sense principles and then get more specific. The hardest part of buying a racquet is to find one that you like best. The problem is not that there are not enough to choose from. The problem is that there are too many (Figure 1.1). You could spend six months trying every racquet on the market, each at a few different string tensions, and you might still have trouble finding the right racquet and string combination. In any case, by the time you tried number 100, you would have forgotten what the tenth one felt like.

Choosing a racquet is a process of elimination. You might find that you don't like heavy racquets or you don't like light ones. That eliminates about half of all racquets. You might also find that you prefer a large head to a small one or that you like stiff frames rather than flexible frames. That way you can eliminate about 90 percent of all racquets quite quickly. The best way of choosing a racquet is to spend about half an hour on a court hitting with as many different racquets you can find—the more the better, but at least ten. You will be able to reject half of them almost immediately because they won't feel right. By the end of the session you might find one or two that are pretty good. Come back a few days later and try the best ones again. Then decide. Either buy the best one or try another ten.

If you can't find a club or shop that will let you try ten racquets, then be persistent. Get your club to organize a racquet hitting—like a wine tasting where you can taste as much as you like for free.

Figure 1.1 *Top row: Nine of the hundreds of racquets on the market. Bottom row: Six old racquets, including the outlawed "Spaghetti String" racquet, fourth from left.*

MISTAKES WHEN BUYING A RACQUET

There are several common mistakes that you can make when buying a racquet. The first one is to choose one because you liked the advertisement you saw in a tennis magazine or because some new high-tech feature appeals to you. By all means try it if you like the sound of it, but don't forget to compare it with a few others.

Another mistake is to buy the racquet that feels best in the tennis shop. Hitting the air with a racquet is not a good way to find out how the racquet behaves when you hit a tennis ball. There is no shock, no vibration, and no sense of feel or power when you swing at the air.

Don't buy a racquet because your favorite player uses it or because your friend uses it. Racquets don't do all the work. You have to match the racquet to your own strengths and playing style in order to find one that works best for you. Try the same brand as your favorite player or friend if it appeals to you, but try a few other brands as well.

Players often decide that they want a racquet that is both light and powerful, a perfectly natural choice. Here again, it is better to try hitting with a variety of racquets before buying one. You might find that a 250-gram racquet is indeed light but a 300-gram racquet also feels light and delivers a bit more power.

The last mistake is to buy the cheapest or the most expensive racquet because of its price. Maybe the best one for you is indeed the cheapest or the most expensive, but price alone is not a good way to choose a racquet. There are lots of good racquets in the medium price bracket. The most expensive racquets tend to be the new high-tech models that everyone wants to try because they are new. Sometimes they are indeed very good, but it is really up to you to be the best judge of that.

THREE TYPES OF RACQUET

Racquets can be classified as being suitable for beginners, recreational players, and serious competition players. Different folks have different strokes and benefit from different types of racquet. Serious competitors and professionals generally use a moderately heavy and flexible frame with a relatively small head and narrow cross-section—about 20 millimeters (mm) in the direction perpendicular to the string plane. Recreational players tend to prefer lighter and stiffer racquets with larger heads that have relatively wide cross-sections, typically around 25 to 30 mm, classed as "widebody" racquets (Figure 1.2).

Professionals hit the ball in the middle of the strings about 9 times out of 10, whereas some recreational players miss the middle 9 times out of 10. A big head helps to minimize this problem by keeping the ball well away from the frame. A racquet with a large head has the additional advantage that it rotates less about its long axis when a ball is hit off-center. The advantage of that is that the shot will be more accurate because the tendency for the ball to fly up

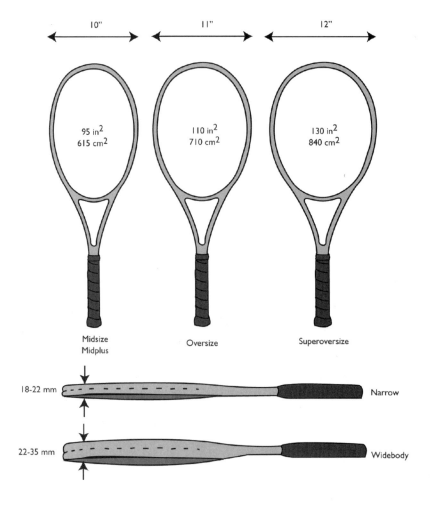

Figure 1.2 *Head sizes and beam widths common in today's tennis racquets.*

into the sky or into the bottom of the net is reduced (see "Twistweight" later in this chapter). The disadvantage for a top player is that it is harder to rotate a racquet with a big head about its long axis. Professionals swing and twist their racquets around much faster than recreational players. A racquet with a big head would slow them down.

There are many other differences between different racquets. For example, there are differences in the number and spacing of the strings, differences in the size and shape of the holes and grommets where the string passes through the frame, differences in the shape of the handle and the head, etc. Some racquets might have a bigger sweet zone than others or are more powerful than others or will give you better control. Each of these differences can be confusing to someone unfamiliar with the jargon or who is not completely familiar with the technical details of racquets.

Equipment selection can be confusing for reasons other than just the racquet features themselves. The player's psychology and belief system about racquets as well as the fit of the player and the racquet are also important.

RACQUETS AND PLAYER PSYCHOLOGY

What a player knows or does not know about the physics, technology, and biomechanics of racquets, strings, and swings influences his perception of what is happening during a shot, whether it is good or bad, what the reasons for it might be, and how to correct or improve on it. A player's knowledge (right or wrong, fact or opinion) that he brings onto the court is the only lens through which he can observe and analyze events. When assessing a racquet's performance, and without any knowledge of racquet mechanics, a player may simply have to rely on trial and error until the racquet performance and player expectations, assumptions, and perceptions all meld into the perfect blend, whereupon the player exclaims, "This racquet is incredible." Of course, what he or she really means to say is, "I have found the racquet that best compliments both my stroke biomechanics and style of play, as well as facilitates the execution of my tactics and strategies." We can determine a "best" racquet in the lab based on certain performance parameters, but that does not mean it is best for any particular player. It only tells you how that racquet is likely to be felt and perceived by a player with a particular stroke and style.

The outcome of any shot depends on the racquet, the stroke, and what the player thinks the outcome is. An example is when players say that string material affects spin and that they get much more spin when they use stiff polyester string instead of a softer nylon. As we will see later in Chapter 4, lab tests have shown that string material, tension, or gauge do not have much, if any, effect on spin. When a player uses a stiffer string such as polyester, he loses power. He thus swings harder, and a faster swing creates more spin. The player then says that the string caused the additional spin, but, in fact, the player caused the spin by swinging faster to make up for the lost power. The player's explanation of cause and effect is incorrect, even if the outcome of more spin is true.

Another example is when players say they get more power from a stiff stringbed, even though it is well known that softer stringbeds produce more power. The possible explanation for such statements is threefold. First, stiffer stringbeds create more shock at impact, and this may be associated with "a hard hit" in the player's mind. Second, because there is actually less power potential in a stiff stringbed, maybe the player will then swing harder, consequently getting more ball speed in spite of the stringbed. And third, the sound of the impact on a stiff stringbed has a "ping" as opposed to a "thud" on a softer stringbed. The ping is more often associated with power. So, the interpretation of the shock and the ping plus unconsciously swinging harder all combine to give the perception, and sometimes the reality, of more ball velocity. But it is not the stiffer stringbed that is doing it, but rather the player's response to the stringbed.

Another example, which is actually the reverse of the one above, is when players say that their strings "go dead" after a period of time. It is true that all strings lose tension over time, but that actually results in more ball velocity, not less, because the stringbed is softer. As above, the player probably unconsciously slows his swing to keep the ball in and also associates the sound of the thud and less shock as indications of a weaker hit. These perceptions ripple effects throughout the player's strokes, shot selection, and tactics. Since he is swinging slower, he is also getting less spin. This, coupled with the fact that the ball stays on the strings longer with the soft stringbed and is thus launched at a higher angle, makes the ball take a higher, less aggressive trajectory, which also is interpreted as less "power." However, again, the lower ball velocity is a consequence of the player's reaction to perceptual cues, which, ironically were caused by more velocity due to the softer stringbed caused by the tension loss.

A classic example of how racquet performance is as much psychology as reality is demonstrated by a blind experiment that showed very few players, satellite tour players included, could discern as much as 20 pounds difference in string tension between otherwise identical racquets. Players were not allowed to touch the strings, string dampeners were used to dull the sound of impact, and players just hit four balls with racquet A and then racquet B. If they could tell that there was a difference, they couldn't tell which racquet was the higher or lower tension. Some might guess one way, some the other. In other words, the immediate feel of power and control in a racquet is not obvious. A player's opinion of a racquet is formed by his interpretation of what he feels, and that interpretation can hinge on the littlest of things that have nothing to do with the racquet's actual performance, such as the sound of the strings. In a sense, the sound tells him how he should feel about the racquet.

One last example is one that demonstrates how players can be fooled into thinking they have hit a ball faster, when they have not. Players sometimes get the feeling that the ball comes off the strings faster than usual or with less effort than usual. The effect is probably psychological rather than a genuine increase in racquet power for several reasons. In general, to hit the ball faster, you have to hit it harder by swinging the racquet faster. The result is usually felt as an increase in the force on the hand and arm. However, you can get an increase in that force just by hitting the ball at a different spot on the strings. Conversely you can get a decrease in the force, for the same ball speed, by hitting the ball in the middle of the strings. A decrease in the force on your arm, for the same ball speed off the strings, might give the appearance of more power, when in fact there is no change in power at all. The only way to know for sure is to measure (a) the speed of the racquet, (b) the impact point on the strings, (c) the speed of the incoming ball, and (d) the speed of the outgoing ball. No one has ever done that.

These examples can be multiplied many times over, but the point is that the player creates a perception of the facts in his mind and acts accordingly. A player can have all the facts wrong but still make all the correct stroke adaptations and be a great player. If you ask that player why he is great and how and why he hits the ball so fast and accurate, you will get a very confident answer, but one that might not be best to pass on to any other player as the how and why of the forehand (though you still may want to copy his forehand).

RACQUET FEATURES COMBINE WITH STROKES

The other complication when talking about racquet features is that they produce different results for different players. When we talk about increasing or decreasing power or control, we are talking about certain properties of the racquet. Put any racquet into a player's hand, however, and the result may be more or less power and control with respect to how and where the player is trying to hit the ball. The combination of any particular racquet with any particular kind of stroke may be complimentary or uncomplimentary to the desired result. In the same way, the "feel" and interpretation of that feel in the player's mind may cause him to change his stroke or tactics in ways equally favorable or unfavorable to the desired result. That is why so many players seem to hold such mutually exclusive and contrary opinions about the power and control of the same racquet (or string).

So, when we say that any specific racquet parameter or feature increases or decreases power or control, we are not saying that the end result for the player will be more power or control, but that independent of any player, the racquet demonstrates more power and control. The racquet is only an isolated entity in the lab, and lab results measure pure physics. A player swinging the racquet changes the conditions under which impact takes place. So, a new racquet will only perform relative to how it interacts with the strokes. The player doesn't change the physics, but the results of the physics might not match the player's intent.

No matter the control properties of a racquet, it has to be brought to the position, speed, and angle that the rebound off the racquet will be in the desired direction. A "true" rebound off a late racquet with "perfect control" does the player no good, and he has no control. A late hit off a "low control" racquet might be perfect though. The player's timing and stroke idiosyncrasies combined with the racquet's "control" will determine the direction and speed of the ball. So, making a world full of perfect control racquets could lead to less total control in the world of tennis, depending on how all these racquets interact with all the strokes.

One thing to keep in mind when choosing a racquet is that all performance variations (speed, spin, and direction of ball) due to equipment changes can be duplicated by changes in stroke. And likewise, small changes in strokes can be initiated by changes in equipment. As such, any change in equipment can either correct a deficiency in a stroke (relative to a racquet), or else require a change in stroke to accommodate the performance change initiated by the racquet. The ideal racquet for a player may be one that is "worse" or less "maximum" with regard to its lab-determined performance properties in order to "optimize" and "integrate" the racquet with the player's stroke.

SELECTING A RACQUET IS ART AND SCIENCE

In light of the factors discussed so far, it is obvious that matching the correct racquet to the player will always be an art, but one that is more and more based in science. Similarly, there will never be one super racquet that fits all players. There will always be 200 models to choose from, and each will claim to have more of something or other than the competition. But "more" is not always more to a certain player. The player will choose the racquet that "feels" best, and he will then make up any number of performance reasons to justify his choice. Because the player has a vested interest in his racquet selection, some attention should be directed toward the care of the racquet.

CARE OF RACQUETS

Modern racquets are fairly rugged and don't need special care, unless you happen to be a good tennis player. The point here is that average tennis players tend to remain average regardless of what racquet they use, while good players need good racquets to compete at a serious level. At the elite and professional level, the care of a racquet is something that is so important that players often pay other people to look after them.

The most important aspect is usually the strings, because strings tend to wear out quickly and lose their fresh new feel, especially in the hands of a professional. Professionals change their strings almost every day, while recreational players tend to play with the same set of strings until they break. If you are a serious tennis player, you should be restringing your racquet at least twice a year. A much better indicator of when you should restring is when the stringbed stiffness drops twenty to thirty percent from its freshly strung value. A good stringer can help you with that. You should own at least two racquets so that you are never without one, even if you break a string.

What else can you do to keep your racquet in top shape? One thing to do is never store your racquet in a hot car. Ten minutes in a really hot car will drop the string tension by at least a few pounds, permanently. The string tension will rise a fraction in winter, or in a fridge, but it won't rise back to the tension before you cooked the strings. If you travel overseas with your racquet, take it on board the plane with you (if you are allowed). Ten minutes on the tarmac will ruin your string tension, and it might even soften the frame. Ideally you should string your racquet when you arrive, not before you leave.

Some other basic care principles are these:

 • Replace the grip when it is worn or cover it with an over-grip.

 • Don't let natural gut strings get wet.

 • Keep the strings straight and parallel. That way the ball can't find a funny spot to rebound off at a strange angle.

 • If you break a string, remove or loosen all the strings immediately. A broken string allows the frame to pull out of shape. After an hour or two it may pull so much out of shape that it will crack, in which case you can throw the whole racquet away. Even if it doesn't crack, it is not a good idea to let it pull out of shape.

 • Don't smash your racquet onto the court. Punch yourself in the head instead, or kick a fence post. Or, better still, learn to control yourself. Watch some professionals play. It is amazing how many mistakes they make. If they can make mistakes, then so can you. It is disappointing to make a mistake, but throwing a tantrum demonstrates to others that you are a bit weird and out of touch with the real world.

Let's now turn the various properties that players are looking at when they are selecting racquets.

RACQUET PROPERTIES

We have talked a lot about general principles and perceptions when choosing a racquet, but what specifically is behind our perceptions and choices? What about weight, balance, swingweight, flex, shock, vibration, dwell time, sweetspots, etc., and their affect on power, control, and feel? We will discuss each of these and more. But in case this list of racquet properties and consequences seems daunting, rest assured that integrating the racquet and stroke into the perfect combination becomes a bit easier when you realize that there are a couple of common denominators in all racquet technologies and their attendant benefits. All racquet performance technologies boil down to two things—altering the stiffness of the frame (and stringbed) and the amount and distribution of weight. That's all. These in turn determine the power, control, and feel. There are seemingly hundreds of technologies in the marketplace, but virtually every one of them is in some way directly or indirectly addressing weight and stiffness. But weight and stiffness can be combined in so many different ways that each racquet feels different from the next. It all depends on how much weight you put where and how stiff that material makes the frame. Knowing this, it is a lot easier to compare racquets by assessing the weight- and stiffness-related consequences of any new technology as compared to another. Often, weight-related technologies can be approximated simply by adding lead weight.

Similarly, any technology or design that affects the stringbed stiffness can often be approximated by raising or lowering tension, which, along with material and gauge, changes the stringbed stiffness. Any effects on the stringbed of bigger headsize, large grommets, free moving string, extended strings, spring-loaded strings, cushioned strings, etc., can be approximated by raising or lowering tension. Most of these technologies are designed to soften the stringbed for any given tension compared to an identical racquet without them. You can do the same thing by keeping your present racquet and lowering the tension.

The same is true with the strings themselves. Any change in playing performance (not including durability) due to a change in material, construction, gauge, or pattern can be approximated by raising or lowering tension. All stringbed and string technologies alter the force and time of impact. That is all. This is accomplished by changing the stringbed stiffness. It does not matter how you change the stringbed stiffness, only that you do. Stiffness is stiffness no matter how you get there.

At the risk of putting the carriage before the horse, we will first discuss the benefits—power and control—before we discuss the features—weight and stiffness. It's just more interesting to know where we are going and work backward than to work our way up to an unknown destination.

POWER

Power is probably the most talked about characteristic of racquets. Manufacturers talk about "ultimate power," players marvel at the feel of effortless propulsion, and the governing bodies cringe at the prospect of faster and faster serves ruining the nature of the game. In the tennis vernacular, "power" is generally used to mean one of two things—ball speed off the racquet or the ability of the racquet to make the ball go fast. Thus you will hear players say,

"This racquet hits with a lot of power," or "This racquet has a lot of power." Such usage of the word "power" is not the scientific meaning at all and can cause a lot of confusion when people who are unfamiliar with tennis vocabulary try to make heads or tails out of players' conversations or what is written in the literature. When a player says, "I want a racquet with a lot of power," he means one that can make the ball go very fast. The belief is that the racquet has a property called "power" and that some racquets have more of it than others. In a sense this is true, but the problem is that there is a large amount of misinformation and confusion when it comes to nailing down exactly what racquet power is and what affects it and by how much.

With those difficulties in mind, we boldly go forth to try to shed some light on the ubiquitous but misunderstood concept of racquet power. To do so, we need to define some terms. Some of these terms we have had to coin ourselves because there is no player-friendly vocabulary, and most of the terms available for use in discussion are intimidating scientific terms that have no meaning to players. So if we use a term as if it is common parlance, it most probably is not the case at all, at least not yet. On the other hand, some words may be used in common parlance, but we define them slightly differently so that they have a precise meaning with respect to power. The vocabulary of power consists of the following words and phrases (Figures 1.3-1.7 will show these terms in action):

> **Power:** The racquet's intrinsic ability to hit the ball fast for a given effort.
>
> **Incoming ball speed:** the speed of the incoming ball just before it hits the racquet strings.
>
> **Relative impact speed:** Incoming ball speed plus racquet speed.
>
> **Impact point:** The contact point on the racquet where the ball and racquet collide.
>
> **Racquet speed:** the speed of the impact point on the racquet immediately before the racquet hits the ball.
>
> **Rebound speed:** how fast the ball rebounds from the surface of the strings, relative to the racquet speed before impact.
>
> **Rebound power:** the ratio of the ball's rebound speed to the

relative impact speed at any given impact point (usually measured using a stationary racquet).

Exit speed: the speed of the ball when it leaves the strings. It is composed of the rebound speed plus the racquet speed.

Swing speed: the angular speed of the racquet in degrees per second as it is swung in an arc centered at some point of rotation such as the wrist, elbow, or shoulder.

Maximum rebound point: that spot on the racquet from which the ball rebounds fastest off a *stationary* racquet.

Maximum power point: that point on the racquet from which the exit speed is greatest off a *swinging* racquet.

THE COMPONENTS OF "POWER": EXIT SPEED, REBOUND SPEED, RACQUET SPEED

There are two components to the speed of the ball off the racquet—the rebound speed and the racquet speed. Essentially, the ball rebounds at a certain speed from a platform moving at its own speed. You add those two speeds together, and you have the exit speed of the ball off the strings. The rebound speed is determined by the racquet's structure, and the racquet speed is the result of the player's ability to swing the racquet. Most people have difficulty conceptualizing the separation of a hit into these two components, so a little explanation is necessary.

The rebound speed is very simply demonstrated (Figure 1.3). If you drop a ball from, say, 20 inches onto a specific location of a stationary hand-held racquet (this is a requirement), it will rebound a certain height. The ratio of the rebound height to the drop height gives the fraction of energy return. If you take the square root of that fraction, you have the ratio of rebound speed to the impact speed. This ratio is usually about 0.4 (times 100 equals 40 percent) for an impact in the middle of the strings (a little more for a heavier racquet, a little less for a lighter one). This means that the ball will rebound with 40 percent of the speed that it had just before impact. The higher the ratio, the more rebound speed the racquet imparts at that impact location. If the rebound speed ratio of Racquet A is 0.4 and that of Racquet B is 0.43, then Racquet B has a more "powerful" rebound component at that impact point. For that reason, from now on we will refer to the rebound speed ratio as the "rebound

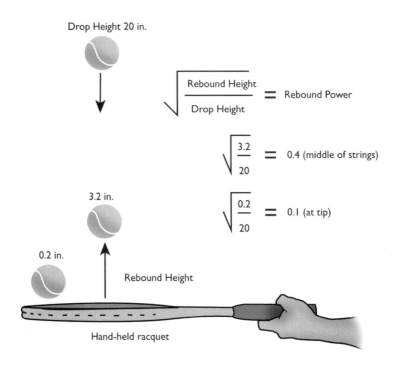

Figure 1.3 *The ratio of the rebound height to the drop height is the energy return. So, 3.2/20 = .16, which means that 16 percent of the energy is returned on the rebound in the middle of the strings above. The square root of this number, 0.4, is the ratio of the exit speed to the incoming speed of the ball. The scientific name for this ratio is "Apparent Coefficient of Restitution." We will call it "Rebound Power."*

power" of the racquet ("rebound power" being preferable to the scientific term which is "Apparent Coefficient of Restitution," or "ACOR").

Rebound power is the amount of power "built into" the racquet by the manufacturer. The ultimate amount of power you can generate will depend on your ability to swing it, but rebound power is what players look for (probably without realizing it) when they go to a shop in search of a powerful racquet. Rebound power varies for each location on the racquet. The location with the highest rebound is also the spot with the fastest rebound. This spot can be called the "maximum rebound point" (as we will see below, this is not necessarily the spot of maximum exit ball speed, however). It is usually located in the throat region of the racquet. Rebound power depends mainly on the weight of the racquet and how it is distributed around the frame and in the handle. Rebound power increases with racquet weight, and it is larger when the rac-

Match Point Box 1.1

Effect of Grip Firmness on Power

The height of the bounce in Figure 1.3 does not depend on how tight you hold the handle. Consequently, you cannot get any more power out of a racquet by squeezing it tight. In fact, the rebound speed and rebound power is the same regardless of whether the racquet is hung vertically on the end of a length of string (the ball being projected horizontally) or whether the handle is held in a vice or clamped firmly on the edge of a table by hand. This result is very surprising and is not what you would expect, but it has a logical and interesting explanation. That is, the racquet bends locally in the impact area when struck by the ball, creating a bending wave that travels toward the end of the handle. The wave reflects off the far end of the handle and travels back to the impact point, but the ball bounces before the wave completes its round trip. Consequently, the size of the reflected wave has no effect on the rebound of the ball. The method used to grip the handle affects the size of the reflected wave, but if the wave arrives after the ball bounces, then it can have no effect on the ball.

The time taken for the wave to travel up to the end of the handle and back to the impact point is typically about 5 or 6 ms, but the ball is on the strings for only about 5 ms. The round trip travel time determines the vibration frequency of the frame. If one round trip takes $1/100 = 0.01$ seconds, then the racquet vibrates at 100 Hz or 100 times per second. If the round trip takes $1/200 = 0.005$ sec, then the vibration frequency is 200 Hz. The time for one round trip depends on the mass and stiffness of the racquet, in essentially the same way that the speed of a transverse wave on a guitar or tennis string depends on its mass and string tension. Thick or heavy strings at low tension vibrate at low frequency, while thin strings at high tension vibrate at a higher frequency. Heavy strings at high tension or light strings at low tension vibrate at intermediate frequencies.

quet is head heavy (like a baseball bat) rather than handle heavy. It also increases slightly as the frame stiffness increases. String tension has an even smaller effect. Rebound power increases slightly as string tension decreases. Near the tip it is usually about 0.10, and at the throat (near the 6 o'clock location on the string face) it is about 0.5.

The nature of the rebound, and hence the rebound speed itself, is not changed if the ball hits the racquet, if the racquet hits the ball, or if each hits the other. The exit speed will vary, but the rebound speed, or the rebound power, will be the same. When the racquet is moving, the rebound simply occurs off a moving launch platform instead of a stationary one. For example, a ball might rebound from the middle of the strings at 40 percent of the speed with which it landed (rebound power of 0.40). So, if a ball hits the middle of the strings of a stationary, free-standing or hand-held racquet at 60 mph, it rebounds at about 24 mph (Figure 1.4). If the racquet hits the ball instead (Figure 1.5), the rebound speed will still be 24 mph, but the exit speed will be 84 mph because the rebound occurs off a platform moving at 60 mph.

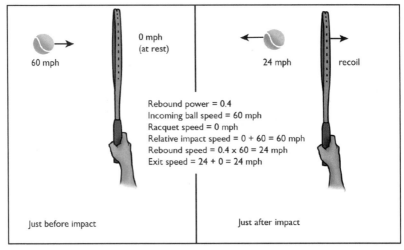

Figure 1.4 *Ball hitting stationary racquet.*

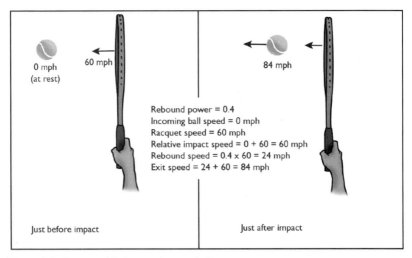

Figure 1.5 *Racquet hitting stationary ball.*

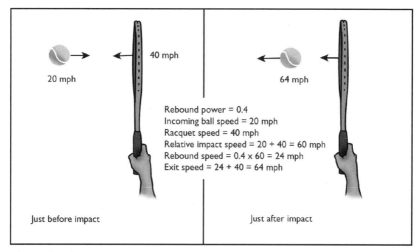

Rebound power = 0.4
Incoming ball speed = 20 mph
Racquet speed = 40 mph
Relative impact speed = 20 + 40 = 60 mph
Rebound speed = 0.4 x 60 = 24 mph
Exit speed = 24 + 40 = 64 mph

Figure 1.6 *Racquet and ball hitting each other.*

If the racquet is traveling 40 mph and the ball 20 mph, as in Figure 1.6, then the relative impact speed is still 60 mph, so the ball rebounds at 24 mph relative to the racquet, just as it did above, to which we add the speed of the racquet from which it rebounded to get an exit speed of 64 mph.

That's easy. Just add the speed of the launch pad at the rebound point (racquet speed) to the rebound speed and you have the exit ball speed.

THE MAXIMUM EXIT POWER POINT
CHANGES WITH RACQUET SPEED

The rebound speed is always greatest at the maximum rebound point if the racquet is stationary. But that does not mean that the greatest exit speed will be attained if the ball hits the racquet at that point. It is ironic that the most powerful point on the racquet is not the best point to hit if you want a shot with the most power. That is because all parts of the racquet do not move at the same speed. On all swings, except very short punch volleys, the racquet is being swung in an arc, which is a segment of a big circle with its center (known as the axis of rotation) located at the wrist, elbow, or shoulder (or even a combination of these, creating circles within circles). Those parts of the racquet farthest from the axis are moving faster than those closer. This is obvious because these parts travel in a bigger circle relative to the axis than do parts of the racquet closer to the axis. However, all locations of the racquet move

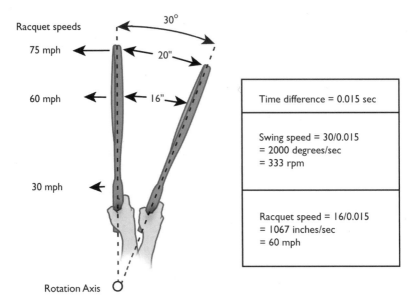

Figure 1.7 *Swing speed vs racquet speed. All points on the racquet move at the same number of degrees per second, but each point moves at a faster linear speed the farther it is away from the rotation axis.*

through the same angle in the same time, so they all have the same angular speed (see Figure 1.7).

It is this angular speed that is properly referred to as "swing speed," and it is defined as the size of the angle that the racquet rotates through per unit of time (e.g., degrees per second, radians per second, or even revolutions per second or per minute). The speed of the racquet at the location from which the ball takes off is referred to as the "racquet speed," and that is defined as the distance that point is traveling per unit of time (e.g., feet per second, meters per second, or miles per hour). That is an important distinction between "swing speed" and "racquet speed."

The ball rebounds fastest near the throat where the racquet moves slower, and it rebounds slowest near the tip where the racquet moves the fastest. At a given location, then, a faster racquet speed can make up for a slower rebound, or a faster rebound can make up for a slower racquet speed. There will be one location where the rebound speed and the racquet speed will combine to yield the fastest possible exit speed. This is the maximum power point for that particular swing speed.

If the swing speed is slow, then the difference in speed between one impact point and another will not be great, and it may or may not be enough to compensate for the loss in rebound speed between the points and thus may or may not result in faster exit speed. The general rule is that the slower the swing speed, the lower in the racquet will be the maximum power point, and the faster the swing speed, then the higher in the racquet will be that location (up to a point, anyway). For strokes of moderate speed and above, that location is usually somewhere between the middle and tip of the racquet head, but exactly where will depend on the swing speed. Technically, the maximum power point changes for every swing speed. However, a general rule of thumb applies: for maximum exit speed, if you swing slow, aim lower; if you swing fast, aim higher.

COMPARING RACQUET POWER

It would seem that if you want to maximize power, all you would have to do is choose the racquet with the greatest rebound power at the location where you typically hit the ball for a certain kind of shot. This is indeed true, but before we can make rebound power our official definition of power, we first must slay a persistent objection to using this power comparison criteria. That objection states that if the easiest and most effective way to increase the rebound power of a racquet is to increase the weight (or more correctly, the swingweight, as we will see later), then the gain in rebound power will be more than lost due to a decrease in racquet speed, and the exit speed will actually end up being less. The answer to this objection is twofold: first, the result of the tradeoff between more rebound power and less racquet speed depends on the stroke, and second, the objection is incorrect to begin with. Let's address each of these.

First, even assuming racquet speed does decline with increased weight, the consequence of this depends on whether the ball is going faster than the racquet or not. The faster the ball speed compared to the racquet speed, the more the contribution of rebound speed compared to racquet speed. So for volleys and slow swings, a heavier racquet with a higher rebound power at the impact point will likely add to exit speed, even if the racquet speed is less. For very fast swings and serves, any slowing of the racquet due to extra weight will likely decrease the final ball speed. Table 1.1 shows these relationships.

In general, the slower you swing compared to the incoming ball, the proportionately more important is rebound power (and hence weight) to your exit speed. Or, in other words, the slower your swing, the more important to you

Racquet Speed (mph)	Incoming Ball Speed (mph)	Rebound Speed Contribution To Exit Speed (%)	Racquet Speed Contribution To Exit Speed (%)	Exit Speed (mph)
0 (volley)	30	100	0	12
30	60	55	45	66
30	30	44	56	54
60	30	38	62	96
100 (serve)	0	28.5	71.5	140

Table 1.1 Rebound Speed vs. Racquet Speed

The calculations assume a rebound power of 0.4.

is your racquet in the outcome of your shots. The faster you swing, the proportionately more important is the racquet speed. Or, in other words, the faster you swing, your racquet is less important to the speed of your shots. It is also true for any given player that he or she would probably do better with a heavier racquet for volleys (ignoring maneuverability), a moderate weight racquet for groundstrokes, and a lighter racquet for serves. Unfortunately you can't change your racquet between shots.

The second part of the answer to the objection is the more important—the racquet does not slow down enough to cancel gains in rebound power and cause exit speed to decline. This is true for three reasons: (1) except for a first serve, the player can almost always swing faster if he wants to, (2) it has been experimentally shown that the actual decline in racquet speed with a heavier racquet is quite small, and (3) the increase in rebound speed and decline in racquet speed virtually cancel each other. As a result, for any given effort, there is little or no decline in exit speed for an increase in weight within the range of racquet weights on the market. And if there is, the player can swing with slightly greater effort anyway. The reason is that the main constraint in swinging faster is the weight (swingweight) of the arm, not of the racquet. The difference in weights between any two racquets is relatively very small compared to the weight of the arm and thus has very little influence on racquet speed.

In fact, experiments have shown that the racquet speed varies as $1/(\text{swingweight})^{0.27}$ for maximum effort swings. Consequently, if the swingweight of a racquet is doubled (e.g., from 300 to 600 grams) then the maximum swing speed decreases by only about 17 percent. A similar effect occurs when throwing balls of different weight. If you can throw a 57-gram tennis ball at 60 mph, then you can throw a 145-gram baseball at about 55 mph, even though it is 2.5 times heavier than a tennis ball. Your throw speed is limited mainly by the weight of your arm, which is a lot heavier than a tennis ball or a baseball and therefore has a much larger swingweight. (See Match Point Box 1.2 for more discussion on the influence of weight on swing speed.)

We are now able to state what is meant by racquet power when you are comparing one racquet to another.

RACQUET POWER DEFINED AS REBOUND POWER

Because, for most any given racquet, you *can* change your swing speed for any given shot situation, and because you *must* change your swing speed in different situations (i.e., serve, volley, groundstroke, etc.), and because the actual effect on swing speed of a change in weight is small, we will consider the properties of the racquet that increase the rebound power as being most important in the racquet's contribution to power in actual game situations. Except in an all-out first serve, those properties that make the racquet easier or harder to swing tend to be ignored or overridden by the player, and thus are not properties that dictate certain power results without exception, as rebound power does.

The major benefit of using rebound power as the prime indicator of power is that it is independent of effort, swing speed, and stroke situation. It is independent of the ability, style, technique, and temperament of the player. So, however fast you choose to swing your racquet, and whatever effort it may take, the racquet with the greatest rebound power will usually hit the ball fastest (except for a maximum effort serve, as explained in Match Point Box 1.2). If you want to hit the ball even faster, then simply swing faster, because there is nothing stopping you from doing so, except the need to get the ball in the court. Rating racquet power by rebound power is not perfect, but it is the most practical and useful measurement considering the way most players actually use and interact with their racquets. We are leaving swing speed up to the player and considering the racquet mainly as a rebound platform. Because most of the time the player has a "swing speed override" option at his or her disposal, we will consider the racquet's contribution to power in terms of its rebound power.

Maximum Effort Power

Even though rebound power provides a convenient measure of the intrinsic power of a racquet, and even though players tend to adjust their swing speed to suit the shot that they are trying to make, the question arises as to how much power a given racquet can deliver when the player uses all the effort he or she can muster. In that case, not only rebound power, but also swingweight, will determine the final ball speed. That is the sort of power that tennis authorities are worried about. If someone can make a racquet that is so powerful that 150 mph serves become common, then the game of tennis will be in trouble. It is doubtful that this will ever happen. That is not to say that a seven-foot giant will not come along one day and belt down every first serve at 150 mph or so. But what if your average six-foot weakling could do it? Even if he could, then it is likely that 95% of first serves would then be a fault because the margin for error would shrink almost to zero.

We have done some interesting calculations concerning the variation of racquet power with racquet weight or swingweight for any player, based on the assumption that the player exerts maximum or near maximum effort. These calculations

are shown in Figures 1.8 and 1.9 for a player who we call Joe. Joe is strong, but not super strong. He is using various racquets that vary in weight and swingweight, but each is 69 cm long, and each has a balance point 353 mm from the end of the handle, so the racquets are equally head-heavy. The racquets are strung with the same string at the same tension and have the same headsize and stiffness. In that case, the swingweight is proportional to the racquet weight. If the racquet weight is doubled, then so is the swingweight. Rebound power also increases as racquet weight increases, but it is not exactly proportional to racquet weight. It is relatively easy to calculate rebound power for an impact in the middle of the strings because energy losses due to frame vibrations can then be ignored. The result is shown in

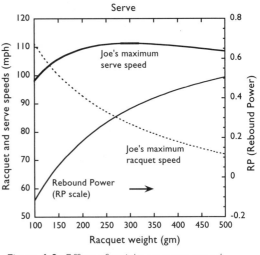

Figure 1.8 Effect of weight on serve speed.

Match Point Box 1.2 continued

both Figures 1.8 and 1.9. For example, doubling the racquet weight from 200 grams to 400 grams will increase the rebound power from 0.17 to 0.44 for an impact with a 57-gram tennis ball.

Serve. Experiments show that swing speed decreases as swingweight increases for a maximum effort swing, as in a first serve, according to the graph shown in Figure 1.8. Everyone has a different maximum swing speed for any given swingweight, but if the swingweight is doubled, then the swing speed will decrease by about 17 percent for all players, at least for racquets between 100 grams and 500 grams in weight. Doubling the racquet weight from 10 grams to 20 grams will make no measurable difference at all to swing speed, but 17 percent is the average measured result for almost all racquets of practical interest and for a range of different players of different strengths and abilities.

Adding the racquet speed to the rebound speed gives the serve speed results shown in Figure 1.8. The serve speed is a maximum at a racquet weight of about 300 grams, but there is only a tiny drop in serve speed at 250 grams or at 400 grams. Consequently, there is almost nothing to be gained by using a heavier or lighter racquet, at least in terms of maximum serve speed.

Groundstrokes. A different result is obtained for a groundstroke where heavy racquets have an advantage over light racquets in terms of ball speed off the racquet for a given effort. The result is shown in Figure 1.9. Players rarely use maximum effort to hit a groundstroke, so it was assumed in these calculations that Joe used half his maximum effort to swing his racquet at half his maximum swing speed. It was assumed also that the ball was approaching at 40 mph and that Joe hit the ball in the middle of the strings. In that case there is a 10 mph increase in outgoing ball speed when the racquet weight is increased from 200 to 400 grams. Alternatively, Joe could decide to swing the 400-gram racquet upwards at a steeper angle than the 200-gram racquet, in which case the outgoing ball speed off both racquets would be about the same, but the 400-gram racquet would generate more topspin.

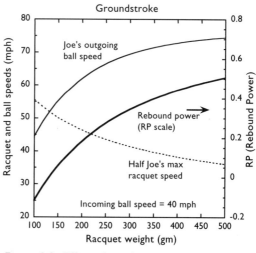

Figure 1.9 *Effect of weight on groundstoke speed.*

Rebound power is the "power" that is available due simply to the racquet's existence and that is always available on every swing, shot, and situation that the game of tennis can throw at you.

REBOUND POWER IS THE SUM OF ALL RACQUET PROPERTIES

The magic of rebound power is that it is the result of the combined influence of all the frame's physical parameters. The effects of the racquet's mass, balance, swingweight, flex, headsize, pattern, string, and tension are each accounted for in measuring rebound power. The rebound is the consequence of the effects of all of these things, as well as every other feature designed into the construction and stringing of the racquet. A racquet with a higher rebound has a more powerful combination of these factors at that impact location than a racquet with a lower rebound. If you had a map of the stringbed showing the rebound power value at one-inch locations radiating out from the center of the racquet, you could compare the power of every racquet in the area of your impact zone (indicated by where you find ball fuzz on the strings of your racquet).

Such a rebound power map shows the results of the different flow of energy in a racquet for each impact location. When the ball strikes a stationary, free-standing or hand-held racquet, the energy of the ball is divided between racquet translation (linear motion), rotation, twisting, and bending. Each of these motions siphons off energy, making it unavailable for propelling the ball. The energy that is left over (elastic energy stored in the stretched string and compressed ball) is used to rebound the ball off the strings, though about 25 percent of that energy is lost in the process also. In general, lighter, more flexible racquets and stiffer stringbeds result in more energy being wasted and less to propel the ball. Also, as you move out from the center of the stringbed, rebound power declines, more so for smaller head racquets than larger ones.

Rebound power is actually tricky to measure accurately without special equipment, but the concept is incredibly simple, and quickly lays to rest any "which racquet is more powerful" debates. It is astonishing that the intrinsic, off-the-shelf power of the racquet at any given stringbed location is revealed so completely and accurately by such an unimpressive, simple, slow collision as the drop test shown in Figure 1.3. No on-court, "realistic" situations are necessary to determine a racquet's built-in power—the power that is available in every single hit of the ball, independent of swing speed.

Match Point Box 1.3

Maximum Theoretical Ball Speed

If the racquet was perfect and lost no energy, and if the ball was also perfect and lost no energy, then the maximum possible serve speed to racquet speed ratio would be 2.0. In other words, the serve speed would be twice the racquet speed. It is impossible to do any better than that according to the laws of physics, no matter what is done to improve the racquet frame or the strings. However, the factor of 2.0 here also requires the racquet to be infinitely heavy. Such a racquet would sink to the center of the earth as soon as it was constructed, and it would suck in the sun and the moon while it was at it. For racquets around 300 or 400 gm, and for perfect racquets and balls, the maximum theoretical serve speed to racquet speed ratio is around 1.5. In practice, the serve speed to racquet speed ratio is typically about 1.4. Modern racquets are therefore almost as powerful as they can be, given that the rules specify that balls must lose energy in every collision.

That being said, the easiest way to hit the ball faster is still simply to swing faster. Every player has more in reserve than any amount of fiddling with the rebound power can deliver. But for any given racquet, the rebound power is the way to compare racquet power.

POWER AND ENERGY LOSS

"More powerful" actually means less energy loss. So, although racquet advertisements are constantly singing the praises of "more powerful" racquets, these racquets have no propulsion system. All the energy that is possible is present before the impact. That is the energy of motion in the racquet and ball approaching each other. The impact does not produce energy; it only loses it. Designing a powerful racquet is *all* about limiting energy loss, not about producing energy. And that is what is measured in rebound power. The primary reason the ball rebounds faster on a racquet with a high rebound power is that the extra weight limits these extraneous motions and thus creates a more stable platform from which the rebound can take place.

If you lay a racquet on the court and put your foot on the throat area so that racquet can't recoil or vibrate, then the rebound power will increase to about 0.9. That is, the ball will bounce to about 80 percent of the drop height (rebound power is the square root of the bounce height ratio). This provides a rather dramatic demonstration of the fact that rebound power is strongly affected by recoil and vibration of the racquet frame, each of which take energy away from the ball. It also shows that the strings play a very important role in reducing energy loss in the ball. If the ball is dropped on the court instead of the strings, then the ball will bounce to only about 55 percent of the drop height. The strings don't supply any extra energy to the ball, even though it might appear that they do. Rather, the strings act to soften the impact. As a result, the force on the ball is reduced, so the ball compresses by a smaller amount and loses a smaller amount of energy. At the same time, 95 percent of the energy required to stretch the strings is given back to the ball when the strings spring back to their original position.

THE BAD NEWS: REBOUND POWER VALUES AREN'T READILY AVAILABLE

The problem is that rebound power is not a published parameter listed in manufacturers' marketing materials or on the point-of-sale "face card" that is attached to the racquet head in the store. This is unfortunate because a standardized rebound power map at selected intervals from the center of the stringbed would give players an accurate, quantitative way to compare racquets. It would show the most powerful locations on the racquet and how rapidly the power deteriorates as you hit outside of the middle of the string face. Instead, players must rely on hyperbolized marketing—"ultimate power"—or, all too often, the uninformed, opinionated recommendations of the store's school-vacation sales staff.

The other, better, alternative is to make judgments of what rebound power is likely to be compared to another racquet based on the racquet features that comprise them—weight, stiffness, balance, headsize, etc. In general, more weight, more weight located farther toward the ends and sides of the racquet (higher swingweight, higher balance, and larger/wider headsize), and stiffer flex all contribute to greater rebound power. Also, anything that makes the stringbed softer will increase rebound power, and anything that makes it stiffer will decrease it. Given these generalizations, you can do a rebound test in your mind, visualizing the effect of each racquet property on the rebound. At least that gives you a conceptual framework upon which to make an intelligent decision. (This conceptual framework will be built up much more in the rest of this book.)

CONTROL

REBOUND CONTROL

"Control" means hitting the ball to a desired location at a desired speed. A player uses speed, spin, and angle of ejection to accomplish this. In this respect, the player has a lot larger role in control than the racquet does.

However, there is something that we can call "Rebound Control." This is a measurement that indicates how close the angle of rebound is to the incident angle when a ball is fired at right angles to a hand-held or free-standing racquet face. If the ball is incident at 90 degrees and retraces its path to rebound at 90 degrees, it has a rebound control of 1.0 (90/90 = 1.0). If it rebounds at 85 degrees, it has a rebound control of 85/90 = 0.94. The reason that the angle is not always 90 degrees is that the racquet bends and rotates backwards, so when the ball rebounds, the face of the racquet is pointing in a different direction as the ball leaves the strings. If the ball hits off-center, the racquet also torques like a screw and rotates around the long axis (twists). The combined effect is to change the rebound compared to the incident angle in both the vertical and horizontal directions. There is actually a rebound control value for both up-and-down and sideways rebound angles.

The harder the ball hits the racquet, the more bending, rotation, and twisting will occur. So, the greater the impact velocity, the less the rebound control, but this scales proportionately for each racquet, so you only need the rebound control for one speed in order to compare racquets. This is also true totally apart for the consideration that the faster you swing a racquet, the less control you have because it is more difficult to hit the sweetspot and aim the ball's rebound from the racquet.

The same racquet characteristics that influence power also influence control. These are weight, weight distribution, and frame stiffness. The stiffer the frame in all directions, the less it will bend and twist. The heavier it is, the less it will rotate in all directions when the ball impacts. So, a racquet that has a high rebound power will also have a high rebound control. In a stationary racquet, power and control always go together, and they, in turn, vary with frame stiffness and weight distribution. This is contrary to the usual belief that power and control are mutually exclusive. Of course, the faster you swing, the less control you have, but that is not the racquet's fault.

The mutual exclusivity of power and control is true when it comes to strings, however. The rule here is that the stiffer the stringbed (a combination of string material, tension, gauge, headsize, and pattern), the greater will be the rebound control, but the power will be less. The reason is that even though the force on the strings will be greater with a stiffer stringbed, the ball will stay on the strings a shorter time, with the net effect that the racquet recoils less at impact. Also the ball is on the racquet through a smaller arc of the swing, which, by its nature, is continuously pointing in different directions. These effects combine to create a truer rebound. Soft strings do the opposite. Stiffer stringbeds will result in a higher rebound control rating, but less power. It is here that power and control are tradeoffs.

WEIGHT

Power and control are performance results that derive from the racquet's structure. We have discussed these. Feel is another performance result that depends on structure. We will now turn to the structure of the racquet to see how it determines these performances. We have saved our discussion of feel until now because it is intimately tied into weight and stiffness and the forces that go with them. Feel manifests itself as the perception of weight and balance, as well as shock and vibration and their duration.

WEIGHT AND APPARENT WEIGHT

A racquet feels different depending on what you do with it. Its "apparent weight" seems to change depending on how and where you hold it and in what direction you try to move it. The explanation of the chameleon-like quality is that the "apparent weight" depends on the distribution of weight in relation to where you are holding the racquet and in relation to the axis about which you are swinging.

For players with multiple racquets, total racquet matching and customization would match all the "weights" in each racquet, so they all would feel exactly the same all the time in every possible movement. That is quite a task, as we will see below.

THE SIX "WEIGHTS" OF A RACQUET

The mass and the distribution of the mass determine six important weight characteristics of your racquet. Each one can be adjusted to help or hinder a player's performance. The off-the-shelf value for each of these weights, or their customized values, affect almost everything you feel when hitting a tennis ball, including power, stability, shock, vibration, twisting, comfort, maneuverability, spin, ball "heaviness," etc. As explained below, the names of these "weights" are made up to fit into a tennis-oriented vocabulary. In fact, they are not "weights" at all, but the combination of forces and torques involved make them feel like weights opposing your movements. "Weight" is not even weight. Technically a 300-gram racquet refers to its mass, not its weight. That's because a 300-gram racquet "weighs" 300 grams on Earth, but take it to the moon, and it will weigh only 50 grams on the same scales, though its mass is still 300 grams. Because there are no tennis tournaments on the moon, we will use mass and weight in this book to mean the same thing, even though it is technically incorrect to do so.

With that disclaimer firmly in place, the "weights" the player feels follow.

The four most important weights are:

1. **Weight**—force needed to pick the racquet up by the handle, with the head pointing straight down toward the ground.

2. **Pickupweight**—torque needed to resist gravity and hold the racquet by the handle parallel to ground.

3. **Swingweight**—resistance of the racquet to being swung by the player or by the impact of the ball in a plane perpendicular to the stringbed and about an axis near the handle end of the racquet.

4. **Twistweight**—resistance of the racquet to twisting about the long axis by either the player or the impact of the ball.

In addition, the following two weights come into play also but are seldom, if ever, talked about:

5. **Spinweight**—resistance of the racquet to being swung by the player (or by impact of the ball) in an arc parallel to the strings about an axis near the end of the handle. This is generally only about five percent greater than swingweight, so it is usually just lumped in with swingweight.

6. **Hittingweight**—how heavy the racquet acts at the impact point, also known as the "effective weight." This is different from all the others in that it is a combined result of weight, swingweight, twistweight, and spinweight—all the racquet's resistances to the ball pushing it around.

Why so many? Weights 1 and 6 are actual weights. The weight or mass of an object determines its resistance to motion in a straight line. Weight number 2 is really a torque (a weight multiplied by a distance). Weights 3-5 are manifestations of a physical parameter known as the "moment of inertia" (MOI) which measures the resistance of the racquet to rotation about the axis in question. The farther away weight is located from the axis, the more it increases the resistance to rotation about that axis. The location of the weight is just as important as the amount. The MOI can be measured about an axis through any location on a racquet. It has different values at each location. The higher the value, the more difficult it is to rotate the racquet about that axis. What we have done is taken each axis that is relevant to the player in playing tennis and named that measurement of MOI by the playing characteristic that it most influences. Physicists and engineers would call these different MOI values I_1, I_2, I_3, I_4, etc., but we prefer to give them meaningful names.

Hittingweight is essentially the combined result of the all the racquet's resistances to ball impact and determines how heavy the racquet "behaves" at the impact point.

Generally speaking, when you change one of these weights, you will change almost all the others at the same time. The amount and distribution of weight around one axis changes the amount and distribution about all the others. Many times, if you change the weight distribution to favor one playing characteristic, you may impair one or more others. That is why it is important to consult with a qualified racquet technician to do your customization. You can imagine the complexity of calculating the amount and location of lead weights to optimize each of these weights for a particular player and then to make each of his racquets exactly the same. Members of the USRSA (United States Racquet Stringers Association) have software tools at their disposal with which to make all the necessary calculations, and many are certified to do these sorts of customizations. Let's discuss each type of "weight" in turn.

RACQUET WEIGHT

Weight and weight distribution are the most important racquet properties with respect to performance. The reason is that they, more than any other characteristics, determine the flow of energy when the racquet and ball collide. Together they determine how much the racquet will be pushed backwards, rotate, and twist on ball impact. The greater the effective weight at the impact point (hittingweight), the less these events will occur. And the less these occur, the more energy will be used moving the ball instead of the racquet. That means more power. It also means more control. The more weight at the impact point, the less the racquet will twist or rotate backward and, therefore, the less rebound error that is likely to occur.

The amount of weight determines how much there is to spread around to influence all the other weight types. But it also comes directly into play as weight pure and simple in picking the racquet up and in moving it in a straight line (Figure 1.10). For example, in a punch volley with the racquet head vertical and where the racquet moves almost completely in a straight line, you experience the weight in two ways—holding the racquet up against gravity and pushing the racquet forward. There is no rotation in these actions, so all that you feel is the weight in the normal sense of the word. All the other "weights" that we will discuss involve rotational movement, which is defined and measured differently.

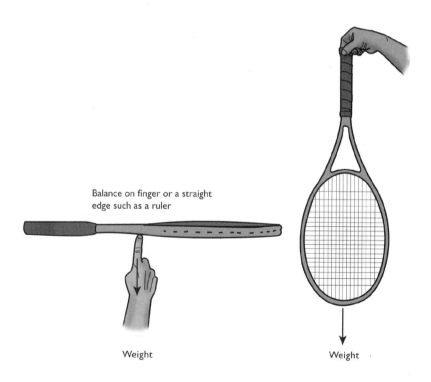

Balance on finger or a straight edge such as a ruler

Weight   Weight

Figure 1.10 *To feel just the weight of the racquet, you must support the racquet from a point where a line drawn perpendicular from the ground will pass through the balance point of the racquet and your support point.*

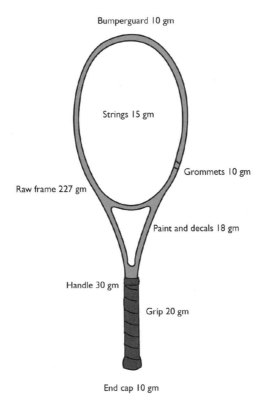

Bumperguard 10 gm

Strings 15 gm

Grommets 10 gm

Raw frame 227 gm

Paint and decals 18 gm

Handle 30 gm

Grip 20 gm

End cap 10 gm

Total racquet weight = 340 gm

Figure 1.11 *The weights of the individual components of total racquet weight. About half of the raw frame weight is just glue (resin) weight.*

The weight of most racquets varies from about 250 grams to about 360 grams, with the majority being around 300 grams. Figure 1.11 shows the components that contribute to the overall weight of the racquet. The trend over the years has been toward lighter racquets because most players prefer racquets that are easy to swing and easy to carry onto and around the court. On the other hand, professional players tend to prefer heavy racquets because heavy racquets are generally more powerful and because professional players are generally fitter and stronger than recreational players.

There is no correct or "best" racquet weight. Even some professionals play very well with light racquets. In that respect you should play with a racquet that feels just right in terms of its weight. Obviously, if you weigh more than 180 pounds, you can swing a heavier racquet than a young child. There is no official rule in tennis about racquet weight. You could use a 1,000-gram racquet if you wanted to, as heavy as a baseball bat, but baseball players don't have to run around with their bat chasing after the ball.

It doesn't hurt to try a heavier racquet to see if it makes any difference to your game. The simplest way to do that is to add some lead tape to the tip and/or the handle or to borrow another racquet. You might find, for example, that you struggle to swing the racquet comfortably, or you might find that you can get a bit more power in your shots. Ten grams added to the tip of a racquet will feel quite different to an extra 10 grams in the handle. The effect is described in the section on swingweight.

LIGHT VS. HEAVY RACQUETS

If a heavy and a light racquet are each swung at the same speed, the ball will come off the heavy racquet faster because the heavy racquet has more momentum and more energy that it can transfer to the ball, and it will lose less energy. However, heavy racquets might not be swung as fast as light racquets. There is, therefore, not a big difference in maximum power between heavy and light racquets. In general, racquets tend to be swung at medium to fast pace rather than maximum possible speed because players need to make sure the ball goes in. In that case heavy racquets offer a bit more power and control than light racquets because they don't need to be swung as fast to achieve the same ball speed.

Outgoing ball speed is a combination of rebound speed and racquet speed. The rebound speed is really a measurement of how much energy is lost in the racquet and ball collision. The higher the rebound speed, the less energy is lost. The energy available to use and lose comes from the mass and the motion of the ball and racquet. During the collision, both the ball and the racquet lose energy. The heavier the racquet, the more energy the racquet has available at a given racquet speed and the less energy it loses during the collision.

Top players are generally stronger and fitter and can make better use of a heavier racquet by swinging it faster than the average recreational player. Conversely, if a player needs to get the racquet to the ball quickly, a light racquet will help. For that reason, even professionals use racquets that are much lighter than they are capable of swinging.

In theory, a heavier racquet should help to reduce arm injuries. There is anecdotal evidence from veteran coaches that arm and shoulder injuries increased when heavy, wood racquets were replaced with modern, light racquets at the end of the 1970s. When you strike a ball coming towards you, the ball tends to push the racquet head backward as your arm swings forward. Alternatively, the head slows down while your hand is still accelerating. Light racquets get pushed backward more than heavy racquets. A sudden twist of the arm or wrist, repeated many times, can result in tennis elbow and other injuries. The problem is magnified by the fact that light racquets need to be swung faster to pack the same punch as heavy racquets, so the impact shock is likely to be greater, especially if you miss-hit the ball near the tip of the racquet or near one edge. Some caution is therefore needed in choosing a light racquet. It might feel great for a few months, but you might notice that your arm is getting sore. If that is the case, try a heavier racquet to see if it helps.

IDEAL RACQUET WEIGHT

In any bat and ball sport such as tennis or baseball, the bat or racquet is typically about five or six times heavier than the ball and about one-fifth or one-sixth the player's arm or arms (Figure 1.12). A tennis ball weighs 57 grams and a baseball weighs 145 grams. A tennis racquet weighs about 340 grams, and a baseball bat weighs about 1,000 grams. One arm weighs about 2,000 grams, and two arms weigh up to 6,000 grams for a heavy man.

There are several reasons for this six-to-one ratio. The weight of a bat or racquet acts to slow down the speed that you can swing your arm. The effect is relatively small for a six-to-one ratio or for any ratio greater than six-to-one. When a bat or racquet strikes a ball, the speed of the outgoing ball depends on the speed of the bat or racquet, and it also depends on the weight of the bat or the racquet. A heavy racquet striking a ball at a certain speed generates greater ball speed than a light racquet swung at the same speed. It turns out that the best weight ratio is about six-to-one. If the racquet is too heavy, then it can't be swung quickly. Furthermore, the ball speed off a 500-gram racquet is almost the same as the speed off a 600-gram racquet. At the other end of the scale, the ball speed off a 200-gram racquet is nearly twice the speed off a 100-gram racquet. But you can't swing a 100-gram racquet twice as fast as a 200-gram racquet to make up the difference because your arm is already about 2,000 grams and limits the speed at which your muscles can swing it.

There is another reason why a six-to-one ratio is about ideal. When you swing a racquet, your upper arm moves first. After your upper arm reaches maximum speed, it starts to slow down while your forearm speeds up. The racquet also speeds up, but just before you hit the ball, your forearm slows down. That way,

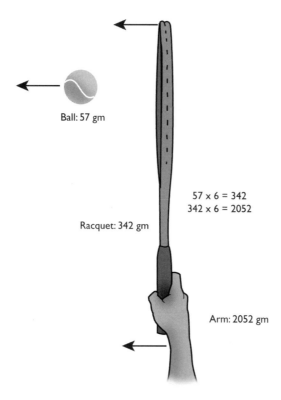

Ball: 57 gm

57 x 6 = 342
342 x 6 = 2052

Racquet: 342 gm

Arm: 2052 gm

Figure 1.12 *Ideal racquet weight. The arm to racquet mass ratio of about 6:1 gives the best flow of energy from the arm to the racquet and from the racquet to the ball.*

energy flows from your upper arm to your forearm and finally to the racquet and the ball. This sequence of events ensures that the tip of the racquet is swung at maximum speed and faster than the handle. A volley requires a different action because the tip and the handle usually travel at about the same speed. The most efficient swing style is one where the forearm is five or six times heavier than the racquet. If the racquet is too heavy, it will tend to lag behind and hit the ball too late. If the racquet is too light, it will reach its maximum speed too early, while the forearm is still swinging rapidly. To get maximum energy into the racquet, the forearm needs to slow down so that it can transfer its energy to the racquet. The action is similar to that of the double pendulum. A golf swing also has this action, as does throwing and walking or running (Figure 1.13).

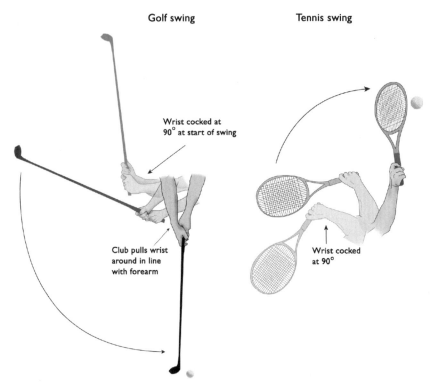

Golf swing

Tennis swing

Wrist cocked at
90° at start of swing

Club pulls wrist
around in line
with forearm

Wrist cocked
at 90°

Figure 1.13 *The arm slows down as the club or racquet speeds up. That way, energy is transferred from the arm to the club or racquet. A tennis serve is like an upside-down golf swing. Each acts as a double pendulum. The wrist is locked at the start of the swing in order to accelerate the club or the racquet, but the wrist should be relaxed just before impact.*

BALANCE POINT AND PICKUPWEIGHT

At one extreme, the balance point of a racquet is something that many players either haven't heard about or regard as a useless technical detail. At the other extreme are professional players who can be very fussy about the location of their balance point. The balance point has a strong effect on how the racquet feels when you hold it in your hand, and it has an indirect effect on the way the racquet feels when you swing it. That's why professional players are so fussy. They bring onto the court five or six identical racquets, each with the same weight and with exactly the same balance point. If one of the racquets has a different balance point, the player will notice it immediately.

The balance point can be located simply by balancing a racquet across the width of the racquet using the edge of a ruler, or a long rod or tube. The bal-

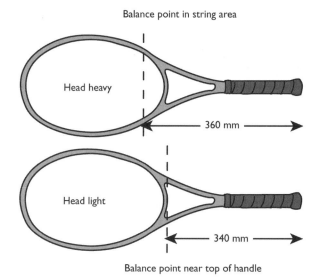

Balance point in string area

Head heavy

◁── 360 mm ──▶

Head light

◁── 340 mm ──▶

Balance point near top of handle

Figure 1.14 *Balance point. If the balance point is more than half the racquet length as measured from the end of the butt, the racquet is head-heavy. If it is located at less than half the racquet length, the racquet is head-light.*

ance point is roughly half way along the racquet and is measured from the butt end of the handle (Figure 1.14). Most racquets have a balance point between 310 mm and 390 mm from the butt end. If the balance point is more than halfway along the racquet, the racquet is said to be head-heavy. If it is less than halfway, the racquet is head-light. If the racquet is head-heavy, it means either that the head is heavier than the handle or that weight in the head has been shifted towards the tip, or weight in the handle has been shifted away from the butt end.

The difference between a head-heavy and head-light racquet is easy to feel just by holding each racquet horizontally in your hand. You can't feel the difference if the racquets hang down vertically. If the racquet is vertical, all you feel is the weight. In a horizontal position you feel a combination of the weight and the balance point. The weight you feel in this circumstance is called "pickup-weight" because this is the approximate position which you pick up the racquet and hold it. A head-heavy racquet will feel heavier than a head-light racquet even if both racquets are exactly the same weight. That's because the weight of a head-heavy racquet is shifted further away from your hand, so you need to use a firmer wrist to hold the racquet horizontal (Figure 1.15). To con-

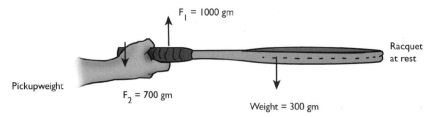

Figure 1.15 *In order to hold a 300-gram racquet in a horizontal position, you need to push up with your first finger (F_1) and down at the butt end (F_2). The total upward force is 300 grams, but the racquet will "feel" heavier than 300 grams because the forces F_1 and F_2 are each a lot larger than 300 grams. That's because the torque due to F_1 (1000 gm x 10 cm distance to butt end) has to balance the torque due to the racquet weight (300 gm x 34 cm distance from balance point to butt end) to stop the racquet rotating.*

vince yourself of this, hold your racquet horizontal and put a weight (your car keys, for example) first on the handle and then at the tip of the racquet.

SWINGWEIGHT

Swingweight is another one of those technical details that a player usually doesn't worry about unless he or she is serious about tennis. Professionals should definitely worry about it because their livelihoods depend on having exactly the right equipment. Even though two nominally identical racquets might have exactly the same weight and exactly the same balance point, they will feel different to swing if each has a different swingweight. Balance point and swingweight each depend on how the weight is distributed through the racquet and, therefore, on whether the racquet is head-light or head-heavy.

Figure 1.16 details a simple example that explains the difference between weight, balance point, and swingweight. Consider a rod that is the same length as a racquet (say 700 mm) and that weighs 280 grams. The balance point will be in the middle of the rod, 350 mm from each end, if the rod has its weight uniformly distributed along its length. It will feel the same to swing regardless of which end you hold.

Now suppose we add 20 grams so the rod weighs 300 grams. Being heavier, the rod will feel heavier to hold. We can add the extra 20 grams anywhere we like, and it will still weigh 300 grams. However, the balance point and swingweight each depends in different ways on where we put the extra 20 grams, and this will affect the way it feels to swing the rod. Consider four cases:

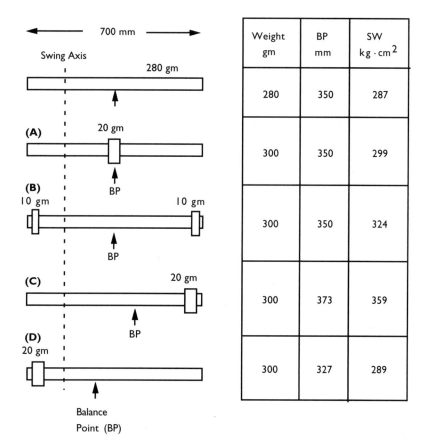

Figure 1.16 *Differences between weight, balance, and swingweight. The balance point is measured from the left hand (handle) end. Adding 20 grams to one end shifts the balance point by 23 mm in cases (C) and (D).*

Swingweight (SW) is always measured about an axis 10 cm (3.94 in.) from the handle end even though players swing about an axis beyond the end of the handle. Swingweight about the player's swing axis is larger. Increasing the swingweight makes it harder to swing the racquet, but it also reduces shock to the arm, improves control, and increases power.

(A) If we put the whole 20 grams in the middle of the rod, then the balance point will remain in the middle of the rod. The swingweight increases when we add the 20 grams because the whole rod is 20 grams heavier. The rod will feel the same to swing regardless of which end you hold because the rod is symmetrical about the midpoint.

(B) If we put 10 grams at each end of the rod, then the total weight is still 300 grams, and the balance point will still be in the middle of the rod. However, the racquet will feel even heavier to swing than case A for a reason we will shortly explain. Being symmetrical about the midpoint, the rod will feel the same to swing regardless of which end you hold. This racquet has the same weight and balance as case A but is harder to swing because it has a higher swingweight.

(C and D) Now suppose we put the whole 20 grams at one end. The total weight will still be 300 grams, but this time the balance point shifts toward the heavy end. In fact, it will shift 23 mm away from the middle of the rod toward the heavy end. This time the rod will feel different to swing depending on which end you hold. If you hold the rod at the heavy end, it will feel about the same as the 280-gram rod without any extra weight (D). If you hold the rod at the light end (C), it will feel even heavier to swing than case B.

If two racquets have the same weight and balance (A and B), each can have different swingweights, and you will have to measure to compare. Similarly, if each has the same balance point and different weights (starting rod and A), you are going to have to measure to determine the swingweights. However, if two racquets have the same weight but different balance points (C and D), the one with the higher balance point will usually have the higher swingweight.

When you swing a rod or a racquet, you rotate it about a point near the handle end. That means the tip will travel faster than the handle. It also means that if you add 20 grams at the tip, then the extra 20 grams will travel faster than if you put it at the handle end. To accelerate the 20 grams faster, you have to push harder on the handle. The 20 grams will feel heaviest at the tip, lightest at the handle, and in between in the middle of the racquet (Figure 1.17).

A 300-gram racquet of length 68.6 cm (27 inches) might have a swingweight of about 340 kg·cm^2 about an axis 10 centimeters from the butt end. The exact swingweight will depend on whether the racquet is head-heavy or head-light. Machines are available to measure swingweight, but you can also measure it yourself by suspending a racquet through the strings and measuring the time it takes to swing back and forth as a pendulum. See *The Physics and Technology of Tennis* for details. When a professional takes six racquets onto a court, the racquets usually have the same weight, the same balance point, the same swingweight, and are strung at the same tension. That way they will not only feel the same, they will also behave the same.

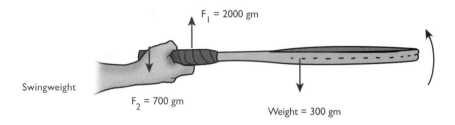

$F_1 = 2000$ gm

Swingweight

$F_2 = 700$ gm

Weight = 300 gm

Figure 1.17 *Swingweight. The sum of the hand forces must now not only support the racquet (as in Figure 1.15), but also accelerate it around an axis at the butt end of the racquet. That requires more force and makes the racquet feel heavier.*

TWISTWEIGHT

Sometimes, when you hit a forehand or backhand, the ball will drop into the bottom of the net. There are several reasons why this may happen, including the fact that you didn't hit the ball hard enough, or you hit the ball downward instead of upward. Alternatively, you may have hit the ball below the center of the strings toward the bottom of the frame. In that case the racquet will tend to twist so that the racquet face points down toward the court instead of facing toward the net. The twisting effect is caused by the ball pushing on the bottom half of the strings. There is no such twisting effect if you hit the ball in the middle of the strings or anywhere else along the axis of the racquet (the line extending from the handle to the tip of the racquet).

The racquet will twist in the opposite direction if you hit the ball near the top of the frame or anywhere in the top half of the strings, in which case the ball will tend to fly over the baseline. The amount of racquet twist increases if you hit the ball farther away from the axis of the racquet. The amount of twist also depends on how easy it is to twist the racquet. In general, light racquets twist more easily than heavy racquets, and racquets with a small head twist more easily than racquets with a large head. In fact, that is one of the reasons that large head racquets became so popular when they replaced wood racquets. Because large heads twist less, it became easier to keep the ball in play.

There are two things you can do to a racquet to reduce the twisting effect. One is to add lead tape to the 3 and 9 o'clock positions on the frame. In other words, you need to add the extra weight as far away from the rotation axis as possible. That will increase the "twistweight" of the racquet. If you add too much weight, the racquet will feel head-heavy, in which case you might also need to add extra weight in the handle. That could then make the racquet head-light, but, in fact, it will actually make the racquet a bit harder to swing, in spite of the so-called "lightness" in the head.

The other way of reducing the twisting effect is to restring the racquet at a higher tension. That way the ball stays on the strings for a shorter time and doesn't push the racquet as far. The force on the strings will be greater, but the net effect of the larger force acting for a shorter time is that the racquet rotates through a smaller angle.

SPINWEIGHT

Spinweight represents the resistance to swinging the racquet up and down as in a chopping motion. This is the direction the racquet moves to impart spin on the ball (Figure 1.18). The axis of rotation for the movement, like swingweight, can be near the end of the handle, the wrist, the elbow, or the shoulder. However, to measure with commercial devices, it is measured 10 centimeters from the end of the handle, just like swingweight. Both swingweight and spinweight are measured by the Babolat Racquet Diagnostic Center (RDC), which can be found in high-end pro and specialty shops. To measure swingweight, you swing the racquet in the machine the usual way, and to measure spinweight, you turn the racquet sideways and run the swing test again. The spinweight is always a little bit more than the swingweight, so it takes a bit more effort to put spin on the ball than it does to hit it flat. Adding weight near the tip will increase spinweight more than adding it at 3 and 9 o'clock.

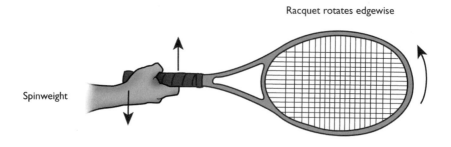

Racquet rotates edgewise

Spinweight

Figure 1.18 *The spinweight of any given racquet is about five percent greater than its swingweight. That's because each bit of mass in the racquet is slightly farther from its rotation axis.*

HITTINGWEIGHT ("EFFECTIVE MASS")

The hittingweight is almost always less than the actual weight. The only exception is if the impact is right at the balance point, in which case the hittingweight and actual weight are the same. The tip of a racquet is the lightest part of a racquet, and the balance point is the heaviest part.

There are two ways to think about this. If you drop a ball on something heavy like a floor, the ball rebounds to a reasonable height. If you drop a ball on something light such as a tennis racquet or a piece of paper, the ball doesn't rebound as high, or it doesn't rebound at all. Because the rebound is weakest at the tip and highest at the balance point (or on the strings near the balance point), then the tip is the lightest part of the racquet. The other way to think about this is to watch what happens when the racquet is held in a horizontal position. Drop a ball near the tip, and the tip moves away rapidly. Drop a ball near the throat region, and the throat region moves away more slowly. Drop a ball on the floor, and the floor doesn't move away at all because it is *very* heavy. Again we see that the tip is the lightest part of the racquet.

The hittingweight can be calculated exactly. In general, the hittingweight near the tip is one third the actual weight; near the center of the strings, it is half the actual weight; and at the balance point, it is equal to the actual weight. The exact value for hittingweight is dependent on the weight, swingweight, twistweight, and spinweight at the impact location. The higher these are, the greater the hittingweight. In other words, it is the distribution of weight that determines the racquet's linear, rotational, and twisting motions upon impact. The more the racquet resists these motions, the higher the hittingweight will be and the greater the ball speed for a given racquet speed at the impact point.

We must remember that for all impacts at any place other than the balance point, it is the hittingweight that determines the results of the collision, not the absolute weight. For a 342-gram racquet, an impact at the center of the strings will be approximately equivalent to a collision with a 171-gram object, and closer to the tip, with a 114-gram object.

As we saw above, as you hit farther from the center toward the tip, the hittingweight goes down. But the tip of the racquet travels fastest when you swing it. Up to a point, the added racquet speed more than makes up for the loss in hittingweight, so the most powerful point on a swinging racquet actually lies somewhere between the tip and the center of the strings.

STIFFNESS (FLEX)

RACQUET STIFFNESS

Modern racquets are deliberately designed to be stiff to reduce frame vibrations. As well as improving comfort, reduced vibration losses act to increase the outgoing ball speed off the tip of the racquet. The ball speed off the middle of the strings doesn't depend on racquet stiffness because frame vibrations are not generated for such an impact. Thus, when you hit in the middle of the strings, there is no difference in power between a stiff of a flexible racquet. But if you hit at a point on the strings away from the middle of the strings, vibration will occur. Stiff racquets vibrate less than flexible racquets because they bend less and, hence, feel better and will have more power if the ball is not hit cleanly in the middle of the strings.

Racquet stiffness increases as the thickness of the frame increases. Try bending a ruler edge-on instead of across the flat, and you will see why (Figure 1.19). Doubling the frame thickness roughly doubles the frame stiffness. In theory the stiffness should increase about eight times, but in practice it is about double. The reason is that the weight of the racquet needs to be kept low, so the wall thickness of the frame (or some other dimension) needs to be reduced if the frame thickness is doubled.

Top players prefer slightly more flexible, narrow frames because the ball is less likely to clip the frame when they tilt the racquet face at an angle to the path of the ball. Players who use a lot of topspin or backspin should therefore avoid very stiff, widebody frames. On the other hand, one cannot make the frame very wide and narrow like a ruler and also have very thin walls because it would buckle as soon as it was strung. The cross-section of the frame is therefore elliptical rather than circular or flat. Widebody racquets are quite a bit longer in the bending direction, making them very stiff.

The stiffness also depends on the type of graphite used to construct the frame, the wall thickness of the graphite tube, and the direction of the carbon fibers in each of the many layers of carbon fiber cloth used to construct the tube. Modern graphite racquets are much stiffer than older wood or aluminum racquets. They are also stronger, which means they can be made lighter and still not break. Part of the reason is that graphite itself is stiffer and stronger than wood or aluminum, but an equally important factor is that graphite racquets

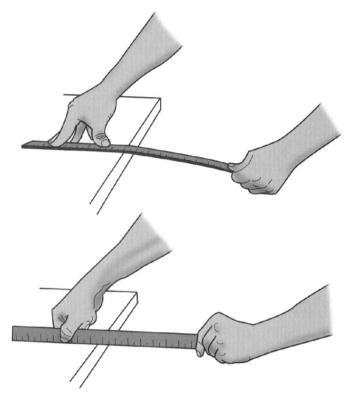

Figure 1.19 *Trying to bend a ruler edge-on is much more difficult than across the flat cross-section. It is the same with a racquet, and that is why frames are wider in the direction at which ball impact forces operate.*

are hollow whereas wood racquets were solid. For any given mass of material, a hollow section is stiffer than a solid section.

MEASURING RACQUET STIFFNESS

Racquet stiffness is usually measured by bending the racquet (by a small amount). For that purpose the racquet is supported between two metal tubes and a heavy weight is placed on the strings or on the tip of the frame. The distance moved by the frame is indicated by a number between about 50 and 85, with 50 being very flexible and 85 being very stiff.

A simple measure of stiffness is the sound made by the frame when you tap it. In order to hear the frame vibrations, you need to place the handle close to your ear, holding the handle lightly at a point about 6 inches from the butt

Vibration Comparison between Racquets

In order to measure the vibrations at the handle, a racquet was suspended freely from a horizontal beam by two lengths of string so that it was free to rotate and vibrate. A tennis ball was also suspended from the beam, as a pendulum, so that it could swing toward the stringbed and impact at the same speed on the racquet and at the exact spot we wanted. An accelerometer was attached to the handle to measure its back and forth motion due to rapid vibration of the whole racquet.

The results in Figures 1.20-1.23 are typical of all racquets in that (a) the largest vibrations of the handle occur for impacts at the tip and throat of a racquet, and (b) the smallest vibrations occur at the sweetspot near the center of the stringbed. The initial motion of the handle is either toward the incoming ball for an impact near the tip, or away from the incoming ball for an impact near the throat. This can be seen from the graphs where the first part of the signal is positive for an impact near the tip and negative for an impact near the throat.

The three racquets shown were chosen because they each illustrate some interesting differences between racquets. Old wood racquets vibrate a lot more than modern graphite racquets and

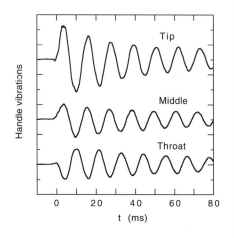

Figure 1.20 *Wood racquet. We missed the no vibration sweetspot for the wood racquet. That sweetspot is between the middle of the strings and the throat.*

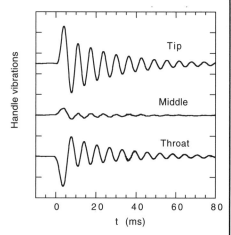

Figure 1.21 *Medium stiff 157 Hz frame with a frame dampening device.*

they vibrate at a lower frequency. Both of these effects are due to the fact that old

Match Point Box 1.4 continued

wood racquets are heavier and more flexible than graphite racquets. The medium stiff frame (157 Hz) is interesting because the vibrations are dampened by a rubber dampener glued between the head and the handle. Additional strong dampening occurs in all racquets when the handle is held by hand. Dampening does not mean that the first vibration cycle is significantly reduced in amplitude. Dampening refers to the fact that the subsequent vibrations get smaller quicker, and it may also act to reduce the amplitude of the first vibration to some extent.

The very stiff racquet (202 Hz) had the smallest vibrations of all the racquets tested. It was also one of the stiffest, and it vibrated at the highest frequency. Frame vibrations are almost completely absent in this racquet for an impact near the throat. The single large spike at the beginning of each waveform is due to the sudden acceleration of the handle when the ball strikes the strings. That cannot be avoided, and it therefore occurs in all racquets. It results in shock but no vibration in the 202 Hz racquet (or in any other racquet that vibrates at 200 Hz or above). With other racquets, the effects of rotation and vibration merge together right from the beginning of the

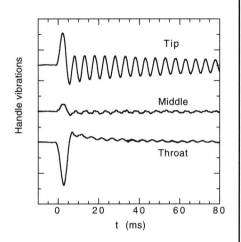

Figure 1.22 *Very stiff 202 Hz frame.*

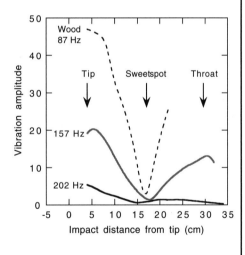

Figure 1.23 *Summary view of racquets.*

impact, increasing the overall acceleration of the handle and the shock felt by the hand.

end. Flexible racquets vibrate at about 120 Hz (one back-and-forth is 1 Hz, or one cycle per second), but most vibrate around 140 Hz, and extremely stiff racquets vibrate at about 200 Hz (wood racquets vibrate at about 90 Hz). By comparison, the strings of a racquet vibrate at about 500 Hz because they are much lighter than the frame and vibrate back and forth much faster. The sound made by the strings is usually described as a high frequency "ping." The frame's sound is not as loud and can be described as a low frequency "hum."

Measuring racquet stiffness comes with a caveat. A racquet has different construction, materials, cross-sections, and mass throughout its length. Therefore, the frame varies in stiffness throughout its length. That means different parts of the racquet will bend different amounts as the bending wave travels up and down the frame. It also means that the speed of the wave will vary—traveling faster in some spots and slower in others. However, in total, the wave's trip up and down the racquet will be exactly the same each time, encountering the same variations in the same places. Therefore, at any given location, such as the handle, the vibration bending wave will arrive back at the hand at exact intervals. If we count the number of times in a second that the handle moves to a peak in one direction, we will have the frequency of the racquet. This tells us how stiff the racquet is overall. It tells us how many times per second the handle will slam into your hand as it vibrates. Vibration is part of what we feel when we hit a ball. But overall stiffness doesn't tell us about local stiffness which influences the direction and amount the racquet bends at the ball impact location. This can affect the launch angle of the ball.

RACQUET VIBRATIONS, SWEETSPOT, AND FEEL

One of the joys of tennis is to hit a ball at high speed with an almost effortless swing of the racquet. It doesn't happen every shot, but sometimes the shot feels perfect. It's more an absence of feeling than a sensation of slamming into something solid. That feeling arises from the absence of racquet vibrations when you hit the ball right in the middle of the strings. If you hit the ball anywhere else, the racquet will vibrate and so will your arm.

A flexible frame bends farther than a stiff frame on impact with the ball. As the ball leaves the strings, the frame springs rapidly back to its original shape, but it may overshoot and then bend in the opposite direction. The frame will then vibrate, bending back and forth rapidly through a large distance if the frame is flexible, but only a small distance if the frame is stiff. The high level of vibration in a flexible racquet adds to the total shock or jarring sensation experienced during impact.

Both ends of the racquet vibrate strongly, even though the handle is held firmly in the hand. The hand is not stiff enough to act as a rigid clamp and to force the racquet to bend and vibrate like a diving board. Instead, both ends of the racquet vibrate simultaneously. The hand and the forearm also shake back and forth when the racquet is vibrating in this manner.

The amount of vibration depends on how hard the ball is hit, how flexible the racquet is, and how far from the center of the strings the ball strikes. When a racquet vibrates, most of the vibration occurs at the tip, throat, and butt end of the handle. There is a spot near the middle of the strings that doesn't vibrate at all. It is actually not a spot, but a curved line extending from the middle of the strings to points at about 2 and 10 o'clock (Figure 1.24). The spot that most people talk about is the intersection of this curved line with the long axis of the racquet. If the ball hits this spot (or anywhere along the curved line), then the racquet will not vibrate at all, even at the tip or the butt end. This spot is therefore a sweetspot, technically known as a vibration node. The farther away from the spot you hit, the more the racquet vibrates. If the ball impacts at a point on the node line near the 2 or 10 o'clock position, then the frame will not vibrate, but it will twist in your hand. Consequently, the sweetspot point on the curved node line is the one that intersects the long axis.

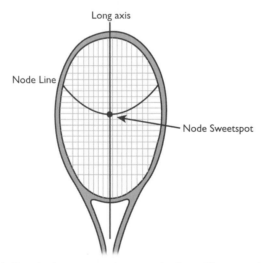

Figure 1.24 *Node line. An impact anywhere on the line will not result in vibration of the racquet frame or handle, but the strings themselves will vibrate. There is only one small spot that has no vibrations and no racquet twist, and that is known as the "node sweetspot" or "no vibration sweetspot." Nearby spots also feel good.*

A racquet vibrates whenever it is struck anywhere on the frame or on the strings, except when it is struck at the vibration node sweetspot. Stiff racquets vibrate back and forth faster than flexible racquets, at a higher audible pitch. It's the same with the strings. Increasing the string tension makes them stiffer and they vibrate faster. It is easy to hear the difference between tight and loose strings just by hitting them with another racquet or with your hand.

VIBRATION DAMPENING

If you touch the frame, you will stop it vibrating almost immediately, in the same way that you can stop a guitar string vibrating by touching it. The hand is the best frame vibration dampener ever invented. Manufacturers usually incorporate other vibration dampening systems in their racquets. This helps a bit and so will a soft grip. But the method that works best is to use a stiff frame to start with.

A long metal tube will vibrate nicely if it is tied to a length of string, like wind chimes, and struck with another metal object. It won't vibrate nearly as much or as long if you stick a cork or rubber bung in one end. That's why vibration dampening materials are often inserted in the handle of a racquet. A long metal tube won't vibrate if you strike it with a tennis ball because the ball itself dampens the vibrations. The same thing happens with a tennis racquet. In fact, if the ball sits on the strings for one two-hundredth of a second, and if the frame vibrates about 200 times/sec, then the ball itself will stop almost all of the vibrations. The effect of ball dampening gets weaker if the frame vibrates slower than 200 Hz, as most frames do.

If a golf ball is dropped on the strings of a very stiff racquet (200+ Hz) in the throat region, then the racquet frame vibrates just like any other racquet (not as much, but some). The difference between a golf ball and a tennis ball is that a golf ball is lighter and stiffer. As a result, the golf ball rebounds off the strings sooner than a tennis ball. Furthermore, it rebounds off the strings before it has any significant effect on dampening the vibrations. A tennis ball sits on the strings long enough to act as a vibration dampener. The longer the ball sits on the strings, the more it dampens the frame vibrations.

The key is for the ball to sit on the strings for longer than it takes the racquet to vibrate back and forth once. A racquet with a bending frequency of 100 Hz has a bending wave that takes 10 ms for the round trip, or 5 ms from one end to the other. If the ball rebounds off the strings in 5 ms, it doesn't get in the way of the wave, so the wave keeps propagating up and down the racquet, and the racquet keeps vibrating. But it takes only 2.5 ms for a one-way trip when the racquet vibrates at 200 Hz, and a tennis ball does get in the way. It dampens the vibrations strongly. A golf ball sits on the strings for a shorter time and doesn't dampen vibrations strongly.

However, the dampening effect depends on where the ball impacts the strings and on the string tension. The impact between a ball and a racquet lasts for about 5 ms—longer at low string tension and shorter at high tensions—and it increases as the impact point moves from the tip to the throat of the racquet. The impact duration at the tip is shorter than the impact duration at the throat. In effect, the tip is lighter than the throat because the tip accelerates away from the ball faster than the throat due to the greater rate of rotation of a racquet for an impact at the tip. As a result, the ball sits on the strings for a shorter time and the dampening effect is weaker. That is why, in Figure 1.22, vibrations are generated for an impact near the tip but not for one in the throat area.

The strings vibrate with a "ping" sound that can be reduced or almost eliminated by means of a string dampener. However, a string dampener has no effect on vibrations of the racquet frame itself. Vibrations are felt by the hand and the arm as a result of the handle vibrating rapidly back and forth. The rest of the racquet also vibrates, but you won't see it vibrating. You just feel it.

SHOCK AND THE CENTER OF PERCUSSION

When a racquet strikes a ball, the racquet exerts a force on the ball, and the ball exerts an equal and opposite force on the racquet. The first effect is obvious because the ball goes flying off over the net. The second effect is not so obvious because the racquet doesn't normally fly out of your hand. It will if you don't hold it firmly enough, which indicates that the ball really does push hard on the strings. The push of the ball lasts for only a very short time, but it can be a very large push. It might be as much as 200 pounds. What you feel is not the ball pushing on the strings, but the handle pushing against your hand or fingers. The result is that your hand rotates backwards about an axis through the wrist, and a shock is transmitted to your arm.

The wrist doesn't bend back very far because the force acts for less than one hundredth of a second. It takes about 50 ms (0.05 seconds) after the impact for your hand to stop rotating backward (about the same amount of time it takes for the racquet to stop vibrating). The impact force between the racquet and the hand is less than that between the ball and the strings because the hand cushions the impact over a longer time. The effect is the same as catching a baseball with your bare hands. You can lessen the shock by allowing your hands to move backwards as you catch the ball. That way you can stop the ball by exerting a smaller force for a longer time. If you don't move your hands backwards, then the ball will slam into your hands with a bigger force, and the shock will be greater, even though your hands absorb exactly the same momentum in both cases.

The same thing happens with the racquet and the hand. The racquet is set in motion by a large force acting a short period of time between the ball and racquet. The hand stops that motion, but it must do so with a combination of force and time that exactly equals the combination of force and time that set the racquet in motion. So, if the force at the hand is less, then it must act for a longer time to bring the racquet to rest.

Heavy racquets, or racquets with a large swingweight, will resist the rotation that causes shock better than light racquets. Racquets strung at high tension will also rotate less on impact, despite the larger impact force caused by higher tension, because the dwell time on the strings is shorter. Hitting the ball between the middle of the strings and the throat area will also minimize shock. The shock force is maximized (as well as the vibration) if you hit the ball near the tip of the racquet.

In theory, there is an impact point near the center of the strings that generates no shock at all. That point is called the center of percussion (COP) and is often referred to as the "no shock sweetspot." If you hit the ball at the COP, there will be a point under your hand where the forward motion of the handle caused by rotation of the racquet will be exactly equaled by the backward motion of the entire racquet. The racquet will then rotate around that point, and there will then be no handle motion at all at that location and therefore no shock. This is shown in Figure 1.25 where the racquet is suspended from the handle by a long string and someone throws a ball onto the strings. If the ball hits near the tip, then the ball will rebound off the strings, the tip will move suddenly away from the ball, and the handle will move suddenly toward the ball. If the ball hits at the COP, the butt end of the handle does not move.

A similar thing happens when you are holding onto the handle, but the weight of your hand and arm stops the handle moving very far. Your hand and arm will jerk in the same direction as the handle wants to move, meaning that there is a sudden impulsive shock force applied to your arm. However, the extra 500 grams or so due to the hand shifts the COP away from the string area into the

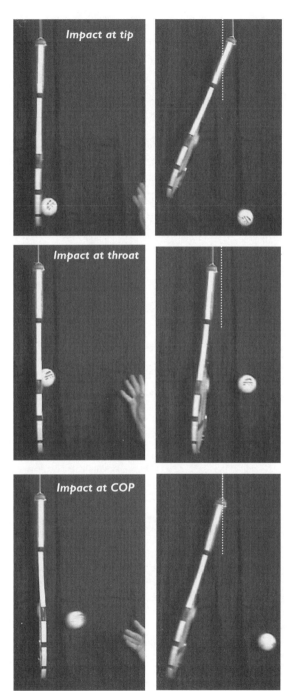

Figure 1.25 Series of photos taken from video film showing the location of the COP. A racquet was suspended by its handle using a long length of string, and a ball was thrown by hand at low speed to impact at the tip, throat, or COP on the strings. The dotted white line is starting position of string and racquet.

Impact at the tip: The handle swings to the right. The ball bounces at low speed and drops vertically downward. The racquet tip moves rapidly away from the ball at about the same speed as the incident ball. Time between photos = 0.04 seconds.

Impact at throat: The handle swings to the left. The ball bounces best here. The racquet tip moves slowly away from the ball. Time between photos = 0.04 seconds.

Impact at COP: The COP for this racquet was closer to the throat than to the middle of the strings. Racquet rotates, but the supporting string and butt end of handle don't move. Ball bounces at slightly lower speed than off throat. Time between photos = 0.08 seconds.

handle region. The COP is therefore not as important to racquet feel as previously thought. The so-called no shock location only comes into play if you are not holding onto the racquet. If you hang onto the handle, then there is no impact point on the strings where you can avoid sudden motion of the handle. All you can do is to minimize the shock by hitting the ball in the throat area. (see Figure 1.26).

The easiest way to see how the shock force works on the hand is to hold the end of a ruler in one hand and push at various places along the ruler. Regardless of where you push, the ruler rotates about an axis in the hand, and the hand bends backward. The force on the hand and forearm reduces as the push location moves closer to the hand because the torque reduces. If you just lay the ruler on a table and push or strike the ruler at various spots, then the

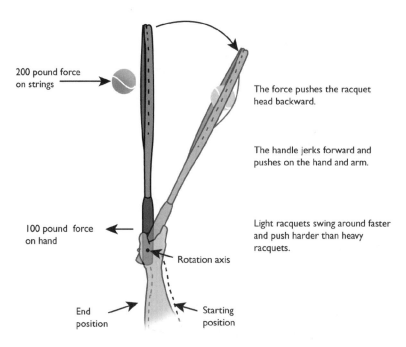

Figure 1.26 *Regardless of the impact point on the strings, the racquet rotates about an axis through the hand or wrist, the hand rotates backward about an axis through the wrist, and the forearm jerks forward. The shock force on the arm is greatest for an impact near the tip of the racquet because the torque on the racquet is greatest there. These events are an insect's view of the action while sitting on the player's hand or the handle. The player sees the racquet moving forward, but the insect sees the hand and racquet move backward on impact.*

Match Point Box 1.5

The Difference between Shock and Vibration

It is hard to pick the difference between shock and vibration when hitting a tennis ball with a modern tennis racquet. A better way to pick the difference is to drop a golf ball or a baseball on a piece of wood about as long as a racquet. A broom handle will work, but a flat piece of wood is better because the ball will bounce rather than slide off the edge. Shock and vibration are then both a lot bigger and easier to pick. You will be able to find a sweetspot about six inches from the end (that is, about one-fourth of the way along the piece of wood) that feels good because there are no vibrations at all. Any other impact spot will tend to sting the hand and jar the arm. Sudden arm and wrist movement is due to the shock force. Rapid vibration of the handle and the arm is a separate or additional effect that you can feel by making it go away when you hit the sweetspot.

"handle" end of the ruler can move in either direction because it is not constrained by the hand.

The force on the hand and arm can be substantial. When a player hits a ball really hard, the force on the ball is enough to squash it to less than half its original diameter. You can get an idea of the force by standing on a tennis ball. The force is around 200 pounds. That force acts for only 0.005 seconds, long enough to accelerate the 57-gram ball to around 100 mph (44.7 m/s). The force on the strings is also about 200 pounds, causing the racquet to recoil. This results in a shock force of about 100 pounds transmitted to the player's arm over a period of about 50 ms as the player stops the rotation of the racquet (Figure 1.26).

How can you reduce the force on the arm? The simplest way is not to hit the ball so hard. Hitting the ball in the throat area, rather than near the tip, will also reduce the force. But most players prefer to hit the ball in the middle of the strings or near the tip. In that case there are five things you can do to reduce the force on the arm, one at a time or, better still, all at once. They are:

- Use a heavier racquet
- Use a head heavy racquet
- Use a more flexible racquet
- Lower the string tension
- Use a softer, thicker grip

By doing all of these things you can halve the force on the arm without affecting the speed of the ball off the strings. Most players these days prefer racquets that are light, head-light, stiff, use strings at high tension, and swing their racquet as fast as possible. It probably explains why more players suffer from tennis elbow and other arm problems today compared with the old wood racquet days. It is fortunate for professionals that they prefer racquets that are heavy, head-heavy, and flexible. That will partially compensate for the fact that they usually prefer strings at high tension. Increasing the string tension increases the force on the racquet, but the force acts for a shorter time. It is not known which is worse—a big force for a short time or small force for a long time—but if the force exceeds the breaking or tearing force of tendons in the arm, then it seems logical that one should reduce the force rather than the time over which that force acts. However, even if the force is not large enough to do major damage, it can do some minor damage if repeated often enough.

The "feel" of a shot results from the combined effect of the shock force on the arm plus vibrations of the racquet frame. It is more likely that arm injuries are caused by shock, given that the shock force is larger than the vibration force, but it is possible that tennis elbow is caused by a combination of shock and vibration because the vibrational back-and-forth "shudder" force on the arm might magnify the effect of a shock force acting by itself in only one direction.

Even though the shock force is so much larger than the vibration, the hand and arm seem to be more sensitive to vibrations, possibly because the vibrations persist for a longer time. Consequently, the spot on the racquet that feels best is the node point near the middle of the strings where vibrations can't be generated, not the so-called no-shock sweetspot at the center of percussion, which has proven to be less significant than previously thought.

CUSTOMIZING A RACQUET

If your racquet doesn't feel quite right, then you might decide it is time to buy a new one. A cheaper option that might work is to have your old racquet customized, either by a racquet technician or by doing it yourself. There are several ways to change the feel of a racquet. Apart from new or different strings or a different string tension, you can also change the grip or add weight to the handle, head, or to some other point or points on the frame. However, before doing that you should inspect the racquet frame closely. The frame might have a small crack, in which case it is time for a new racquet. Sometimes the problem might be that the grommets holding the strings are too sharp and are cut-

---

Match Point Box 1.6

Customizing Weight, Balance, and Swingweight

Changing the Balance Point

A rule of thumb is that 5 grams of lead tape added to the tip or the end of the handle will shift the balance point by about 5 mm, and 10 grams will shift the balance point by about 10 mm. If you add 10 grams on one side of the balance point and 10 grams an equal distance on the other side, then the balance point will not shift at all. The latter technique allows you to increase the weight and the swingweight without shifting the balance point.

Consider a racquet of mass M (gm) with a balance point at distance B (mm) from the extreme end of the handle. Suppose you add m (gm) at a distance D (mm) from the extreme end of the handle. The new balance point will shift toward the extra mass by a distance x given by

$$x = m(D - B)/(M + m).$$

For example, if M = 320, m = 10, B = 350 and D = 690 then

$$x = 10(690 - 350)/(320 + 10)$$
$$= 10 \times 340/330 = 10.3.$$

The new balance point therefore shifts 10.3 mm toward the tip. If you put the extra 10 gm at D = 20 mm, then

$$x = 10(20 - 350)/330 = -10.0 \text{ mm}$$

meaning that the new balance point shifts 10.0 mm toward the handle.

Changing the Swingweight

The only way to decrease the swingweight of a racquet is to reduce its mass. That is not normally possible unless the racquet was previously customized by adding lead tape. If you add m grams at a point D mm from the extreme end of the handle, then the increase in swingweight is given by

$$m \times (D - 100) \times (D - 100)/100,000$$

in the usual kg·cm^2 units.

For example, if m = 10 gm and D = 690 mm, then the increase is

$$10 \times 590 \times 590/100,000 = 34.8 \text{ kg·cm}^2$$

If you added the 10 gm at D = 100 mm, there would be no increase in swingweight at all. That is, no increase about a swing axis 100 mm from the end of the handle where swingweight is normally measured. But players swing their racquet about an axis near their wrist or near their elbow (depending on the particular stroke) so there would be a noticeable increase in swingweight as far as the player is concerned.

---

ting through the strings and lowering their tension. In that case all you need to do is to replace the grommets.

Professional players usually customize their racquets so each feels the same. The point of this is that even if you buy two nominally identical racquets, they will usually be slightly different. One might be 320 grams with a balance point at 340 mm, and the other might be 325 grams with a balance point at 345 mm. A racquet technician will be able to add mass here and there to make each of these racquets (or all 6 if you are a professional) almost exactly the same. Sometimes a bit of trial and error is needed. It is easy to add small strips of adhesive lead tape before a restring so they are hidden out of the way under the bumper strip or under the grip.

Adding weight to the tip of a racquet makes the racquet harder to swing, but it adds power to the racquet head so you don't need to swing the racquet as fast anyway. If your problem is that you hit the ball too early, then adding weight at the tip might help to fix the problem by slowing down the tip. If you tend to hit the ball too late then one solution (besides buying a lighter racquet that swings faster) is either to take weight off the tip or add weight to the handle. That way your forearm will slow down a bit and give the tip of the racquet a chance to catch up. Adding weight to the handle simply slows down the handle end compared to the tip end. To hit the ball properly, the handle end and the tip end both need to be in the correct spot when you contact the ball. That might require a change in swing style or timing or it might be possible to fix the problem simply by adding weight to the racquet.

There is a third location where extra weight can be of benefit. That is, at the 3 and 9 o'clock positions on the frame (the tip being at 12 o'clock). The advantage of adding extra weight at these locations is that it is located farther from the long axis and hence it increases the twistweight of the racquet (see "Twistweight" section).

Further Reading

H. Brody, R. Cross and C. Lindsey, The Physics and Technology of Tennis, Racquet Tech Publishing, Solana Beach, USA (2002).

H. Brody, Tennis Science for Tennis Players, University of Pennsylvania Press, 1987.

R.C. Cross, The sweet spots of a tennis racquet, Sports Engineering, 1, 63-78 (1998).

R.C. Cross, Impact of a ball with a bat or racket, Am. J. Phys. 67, 692-702 August (1999).

R. Cross, Customising a tennis racket by adding weights, Sports Engineering, 4, 1-14 (2001).

R. Cross, Center of percussion of hand-held implements, Am J. Phys. 72, 622-630 (2004).

R. Cross, A double pendulum swing experiment: In search of a better bat, Am. J. Phys. 73, 330-339 (2005).

R. Cross and R. Bower, Effects of swing-weight on swing speed and racket power, Journal of Sports Sciences (to be published late 2005).

Chapter Two

Strings

Many technologies affect stringbed performance, including headsize, string patterns, suspension systems, and string materials, gauge and construction, but ultimately they all come down to one thing—making the stringbed softer or stiffer.

STRINGS AND THE MODERN GAME

To date, trial and error have reigned in choosing strings. Most tennis players use nylon strings. Up to about 1990 most professional players preferred natural gut because they liked its feel and performance. In recent times, most professionals have switched to using polyester strings. The reason is hard to pin down, but polyester seems to suit the modern style of game played by professionals. It is not necessarily the best string for recreational players.

Natural gut is made from the long intestines of cows. It is made from the thin stretchy membrane known as the serosa which surrounds the intestine and which allows the intestine to expand and contract as a cow digests its meal. The intestine of a cow is long enough to string a tennis racquet, but the serosa is too thin to make even a 0.8 millimeter (mm) diameter string. It takes three cows to make a thick enough string for one tennis racquet. (If you are so inclined, you can even go to the butcher and get your own serosa sausage skin and make your own gut.) The process takes a few days of cleaning, twisting, drying, and polishing, so it is expensive. However, the result is a string that is more elastic than any man-made synthetic, and it holds its tension better than any synthetic. The main problem is that it is not as durable and tends to break more easily, especially if it gets wet. It is a string that has a soft feel that some players still prefer.

It seems that modern professionals no longer need the soft feel of natural gut because they belt almost every ball as hard as they can. Polyester is stiffer than natural gut and is also stiffer than nylon but not as stiff as Kevlar (a Dupont product that has become the generic term for a category of materials known as "aramids"). However, polyester loses its tension faster than any other string. Many players say that polyester holds its tension better than nylon, but laboratory tests prove otherwise. If a racquet is strung with a nylon string at a tension of 60 pounds, then the tension will have dropped to around 55 pounds by the time the racquet arrives on the court. The tension drops rapidly in the first half hour after stringing and will drop further as the weeks go by, even without hitting a ball. Hitting a ball many times acts to decrease the tension even further. Eventually, a player will notice that the strings feel dead, meaning that they have lost their crisp new feel and start to feel soggy. There may also be a perception that the strings have lost their power, even if they haven't, because a soggy string will have a soft feel that players will associate with a softish hit. In fact, a drop in string tension acts to increase the string power a tiny bit.

If a racquet is strung at 60 pounds with a polyester string, the tension will drop to around 50 pounds after the first half hour. However, because polyester is so stiff, the strings will feel stiff even when the tension is low. The reason is that the strings stretch a few millimeters when they are used to hit a ball, and hence the tension rises rapidly due to the extra stretch while the ball is on the strings. With natural gut or nylon the rise in tension due to the string stretching is smaller, and the feel of the string depends more on the tension before the string starts to stretch.

Nylon is still the preferred string of most recreational players because it is generally cheaper and more durable than gut and is softer than polyester and Kevlar. There is nothing in the rules to stop a player using a steel string if he or she wants to, but it will feel really stiff, and it will cut the ball to pieces.

In fact, the International Tennis Federation's rules don't say that much about strings at all. They state only that, "The hitting surface of the racket shall be flat and consist of a pattern of crossed strings connected to a frame and alternately interlaced or bonded where they cross; and the stringing pattern shall be generally uniform, and in particular not less dense in the centre than in any other area. The racket shall be designed and strung such that the playing characteristics are identical on both faces." The rules go on to state that, "The strings shall be free of attached objects and protrusions other than those utilized solely and specifically to limit or prevent wear and tear or vibration, and which are reasonable in size and placement for such purposes."

Within the constraints of the rules, all kinds of string patterns and string constructions have evolved. Patterns of main strings and cross strings typically range from open patterns such as 14 mains and 16 crosses to denser patterns such as 18 mains and 20 crosses. The accumulation of tension on the frame from all those strings each individually pulled to 60 or so pounds can be as much as half a ton. That is a force that would crunch an old wood racquet.

Open patterns tend to have more string movement, as do strings at lower tensions. String movement is caused by the ball pushing the main strings to the side. This happens on virtually every hit, but the strings usually spring back to position when they are new. However, dirt and loss of tension can cause them not to spring back. Players like to move these strings back to "square" between points because they can cause unpredictable bounces if left askew. Some players use "string savers" to keep the strings aligned as well as to increase their longevity by preventing the "sawing" of the main strings which can lead to breakage.

Strings come in many materials and constructions ranging from a single monofilament to multifilament strings composed of thousands of separate filaments. Strings with more filaments tend to be softer but less durable, whereas a monofilament would be stiffer and more durable. Some strings are constructed with a center core of one to several larger filaments and with one to three layers of wraps around them for durability. Players choose soft strings because they have less shock on impact and a bit more power. Stiffer strings are chosen because they add to control and many players like the "feedback" from a "crisper" impact.

STRINGBED STIFFNESS

Where racquets are all about control and power, strings are mostly about control and feel. There is a lot of anecdotal information about strings that is the result of 100 years of tradition, experience, and myth. Science has looked into this only during the last ten years. We still don't properly understand why players' perceptions often differ from laboratory measurements on strings, and we don't properly understand what players mean when they say, for example, "I get huge power and spin from these strings." Players, coaches, and stringers fervently believe that string properties substantially affect power and spin, but as we will see, they do little to affect these, but a great deal to affect control and feel. The minimal effects that strings do have on power show up more as control effects and should be discussed as such.

Strings are tested in the lab by taking an isolated length of string (not installed in a racquet) and stretching it to a certain tension. It is then struck with a non-deformable hammer. Tests conducted in this manner are able to determine the intrinsic properties of the string, independent of any influence of the frame, neighboring strings in a stringbed, or ball deformation.

Strings themselves are only one part of the stringbed system. It is the entire system that is important. "Stringbed" is the key word. Over the years, many, many technologies have been developed to affect the performance of the stringbed. They have involved headsize, string pattern, suspension systems, and string materials, gauge, and tension. But interesting, and not often noticed, is that every string and racquet technology that affects the stringbed does so by affecting its stiffness. This is often difficult to realize when the technologies are described in advertisements by such terminology as launch pads, string length extenders, or free motion technologies. But whatever they are called, they come down to one performance-oriented common denominator—making the stringbed softer or stiffer. We will examine how these technologies affect stringbed stiffness and then examine the role of stringbed stiffness on perform-ance. Keep in mind that differences in stiffness and the labels "soft" and "stiff" are not meant to indicate "good" or "bad." Some players will call the softer string "comfortable" while others will call it "mushy." And while some will call the stiffer string "crisp," others will call it "harsh." Also, it is important to keep in mind that much of the recent findings in science are contrary to popular belief. Why this is, is interesting in itself, but it also makes it difficult to com-municate and explain new findings.

STATIC AND DYNAMIC STRINGBED STIFFNESS

Most players don't realize that every choice concerning properties or features of string (except durability) comes down to how they will affect stringbed stiff-ness. Material, construction, gauge, and tension all influence string stiffness, which in turn affects stringbed stiffness, which affects power, control, and feel.

Stringbed stiffness is measured in two ways. Dynamic stiffness refers to how much the stringbed will deflect perpendicular to the strings when it is impact-ed with an object of given energy. That is the most relevant test, but it is also a complicated test, so you will not often see dynamic stringbed stiffness val-ues. The most common method of measuring stringbed stiffness is a static stiff-ness test. This method measures the string deflection when a force is applied slowly (i.e., not a collision-like impact) to a certain area of the stringbed (see Figure 2.1). The deflection is the result of all the stringbed factors listed above.

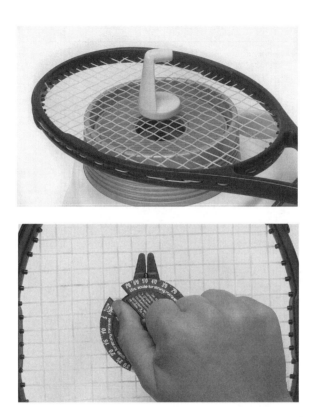

Figure 2.1 *(top) RDC stringbed stiffness measurement. (bottom) A Stringmeter string tension measurement.*

Stringbed stiffness and string stiffness are not the same thing, though the latter contributes to the former. String stiffness is only a measure of the string material and its gauge. String stiffness can be measured in two ways: longitudinally or transversely. The longitudinal, or lengthwise, stiffness refers to how much the string stretches when pulled by a given force (Figure 2.2). Transverse stiffness refers to how much the string deflects when a force is applied sideways to a string, as when a ball hits it (Figure 2.3). Transverse stiffness depends on longitudinal stiffness because in order to deflect, the string has to lengthen. However, interestingly enough, at very low transverse forces, all string materials at the same tension deflect about the same because the stretch is so small compared to the overall length of the string and the tension does not increase much for such a small elongation. But at higher transverse forces typical of impacts with tennis balls, the softer strings stretch more and

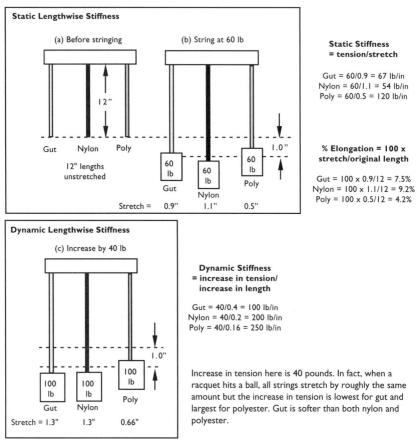

Static Lengthwise Stiffness

(a) Before stringing   (b) String at 60 lb

I 2"

Gut   Nylon   Poly

12" lengths
unstretched

Gut = 60 lb   Nylon = 60 lb   Poly = 60 lb

1.0"

Stretch =   0.9"   I.I"   0.5"

**Static Stiffness
= tension/stretch**

Gut = 60/0.9 = 67 lb/in
Nylon = 60/1.1 = 54 lb/in
Poly = 60/0.5 = 120 lb/in

**% Elongation = 100 x
stretch/original length**

Gut = 100 x 0.9/12 = 7.5%
Nylon = 100 x 1.1/12 = 9.2%
Poly = 100 x 0.5/12 = 4.2%

Dynamic Lengthwise Stiffness

(c) Increase by 40 lb

1.0"

Gut = 100 lb   Nylon = 100 lb   Poly = 100 lb

Stretch = 1.3"   1.3"   0.66"

**Dynamic Stiffness
= increase in tension/
increase in length**

Gut = 40/0.4 = 100 lb/in
Nylon = 40/0.2 = 200 lb/in
Poly = 40/0.16 = 250 lb/in

Increase in tension here is 40 pounds. In fact, when a racquet hits a ball, all strings stretch by roughly the same amount but the increase in tension is lowest for gut and largest for polyester. Gut is softer than both nylon and polyester.

Figure 2.2 *Static and dynamic lengthwise (longitudinal) stiffness. Gut is stiffer than nylon from 0-60 pounds (i.e., during stringing) but is softer going from 60 to 100 pounds (the range of tension increase during a tennis hit). Static stiffness is not important to a player. It is the additional stretch of the strings when striking a ball, and hence the dynamic stiffness, that is important.*

thus deflect more than stiffer strings. More deflection means softer feel, less shock, and a bit more power.

Stringbed stiffness measures the combined effects of many racquet and string elements on the transverse (perpendicular to the strings) deflection of the stringbed. Stringbed stiffness is comprised of many things including headsize (including string length), head shape, stringing pattern (determining the total number of strings), racquet head stiffness, string support system, and the strings themselves. But given the racquet you are playing with, string material stiffness and tension are the most important factors in stringbed performance

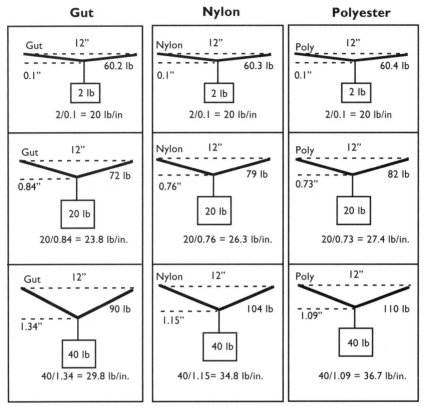

Sideways stiffness = sideways force/sideways stretch

Each string is 12 inches long and at 60 pounds tension before each weight is added.
Average lengthwise stiffness: Gut = 100 lb/in.   Nylon = 200 lb/in.   Poly = 250 lb/in.

Figure 2.3 *Sideways (transverse) stiffness is a lot less than lengthwise stiffness and is the same for all strings for a small sideways stretch (row 1), but it increases the farther it stretches by different amounts for different strings (rows 2 and 3). That's why different strings feel different. But despite that difference, the ball speed off different strings is almost exactly the same because all strings return 95% of their elastic energy back to the ball, regardless of initial tension.*

because they are all that you can change on a day-to-day basis. And when you change the stringbed stiffness, what you are altering is primarily the feel (shock and vibration) and control. As illustrated in Figure 2.4, changing stringbed stiffness (by material or tension) does not have an effect on spin, and it has a very small effect on power.

When we refer to a string's stiffness, we are referring to its lengthwise stiffness as a property of the material. When we refer to stringbed stiffness, we are refer-

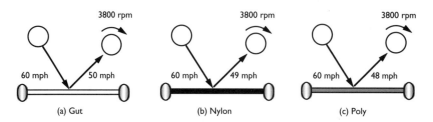

Figure 2.4 *Changing stringbed stiffness by changing string material (or tension) only slightly affects power and has no affect on spin. The main consequence is on feel and control. But because feel and control can affect power, spin, and strokes, many players feel that altering the stringbed significantly affects performance.*

ring to the transverse stiffness, of which longitudinal stiffness is a major component.

EFFECT OF STRING MATERIAL AND GAUGE ON STRINGBED STIFFNESS

String stiffness is a combination of material, gauge (i.e., string diameter and, thus, amount of material), length, and tension. But it is not a single number that is the same all of the time such that you can say, "This string has a stiffness of such and such." The stiffness of the string changes depending on what the tension is before you start stretching it. A string at 50 pounds will stretch more for each pound of impact force compared to a string at 70 pounds. In other words, the string is stiffer at higher tensions, not just because of the tension, but also because of a change in the material property itself. This is a property of all common string materials. A steel string would not act that way. It would stretch lengthwise the same amount for each pound of impact force whether it were strung at 40, 60, or 80 pounds, and you could say that the steel string has a definite value for longitudinal stiffness. But you couldn't say that for transverse stiffness because all materials, including steel, get stiffer in the transverse direction as tension increases. Fortunately, in the normal stringing range of 50-70 pounds, different string materials don't change stiffness radically compared to each other as tension is altered. So, if one string is stiffer than another at 50 pounds, it is, for all practical purposes, safe to say that it is stiffer by about the same proportion at 70 pounds. So they will each feel about the same relative to each other at each tension. However, they will each feel stiffer than they did at the lower tension. The one exception is gut, which is stiffer at lower tensions compared to nylon, but the stiffness stays relatively constant at the ranges of higher tensions caused by ball impact, and it is less stiff than other strings at these tensions as a result.

There are only four different string materials in common use. In order from softest to stiffest they are: gut, nylon, polyester, and Kevlar. These groups have very little, if any, overlap in measured stiffness values from one group to another. There is a tiny bit of overlap between nylon and polyester (but only for a very few strings), as new manufacturing processes have allowed polyester to be softened. Within each category, there is a range of variance, but nothing as significant as the leap between separate categories. Table 2.1 shows the stiffness ranges for all strings on the market in 2005.

Table 2.1 Dynamic Stiffness and Tension Loss		
Material	**Lengthwise Stiffness Range for a 12" string (lb/in.)**	**Tension Loss (after 200 secs & 5 solid impacts)**
Gut	90-119	6.1-9.2 lb
Nylon/Zyex	136-242	6.5-12.2 lb
Polyester	199-320	7.9-18.9 lb
Kevlar	470-981	5.6-10.5 lb

If measured with string twice as long, the string would stretch twice as far, and the stiffness value would be half, but each string would maintain its relative stiffness to the other strings.

The stiffness values are experimentally determined in the lab, and each and every string is a bit different. Because stiffness varies with the string tension and length of the string, each string is measured at the same starting tension and length. For each string, the following parameters can be determined: peak impact force, tension rise, dwell time, string elongation, string deflection (perpendicular to string), impact tension loss, and lengthwise and sideways stiffness.

These values are published by the USRSA (US Racquet Stringers Association) twice a year, and USRSA members have access to the data both on the internet and in printed materials. A qualified USRSA racquet technician can help you find the stiffness of string to meet your needs or can suggest a hybrid mix of different strings for the mains and crosses.

It is unfortunate that string packaging doesn't contain a standardized tested "Stiffness Value." That would simplify life immensely for the player/consumer. There would then be a definitive method for comparing one string to another in its most important characteristic that determines all other string performance values. Just as with racquets, where the rebound power value could be used to definitively compare racquets, the most objective, valuable, and helpful information is not always available. That is not unusual in any industry because getting competitors to agree on industry standards and how they are to be determined is notoriously difficult for the simple reason that quantification demystifies the product and neutralizes marketing hyperbole.

Packaging usually has some 1-10 scale for, at least, power, control, and durability. This can be helpful comparing the strings within a brand's offerings, but not much use comparing among brands. Durability is a separate issue, but power and control each depend completely on stiffness. If you know the stiffness, you know the relative power and control, as well as the likely shock, feel, and comfort characteristics of the string.

Table 2.1 also has a column for tension loss. This is a property of the material and is related to stiffness because it determines the consistency over time of the stringbed stiffness. Every string loses tension from the second it is installed and with every hit of a tennis ball. The rate of tension loss determines how much and how quickly the stiffness of your stringbed will change, and with it, the performance and feel. Figure 2.5 plots the lengthwise stiffness and tension loss data for each string on the market in 2005. The tension loss was measured by pulling the string to 60 pounds, waiting 200 seconds, and then impacting the string five times with a force comparable to hitting a 120 mph serve. The tension loss is thus a combination of static time tension loss and dynamic impact tension loss. Polyester loses the most tension and gut the least.

The rate of loss slows to a mere creep after a couple of days and remains "perceptually" about the same for a few weeks. This means different things to different players. If you are a typical recreational player, the feel you are looking for is the stabilized feel that you experience after a couple of days and then for weeks after. If you are a pro, you need your racquets to feel exactly the same every day. That is why high level players restring so frequently.

EFFECT OF STRING TENSION ON STRINGBED STIFFNESS

Stringbeds get stiffer at higher tension for two reasons: one reason is the tension itself and the other is because string materials get longitudinally stiffer the

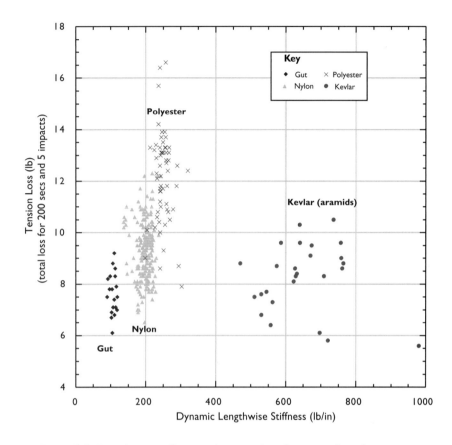

Figure 2.5 *Lengthwise stiffness and tension loss for most all performance strings on the market in 2005. Each material groups nicely with respect to lengthwise stiffness; however, there is a large overlap between materials when it comes to tension loss. It is clear that on average, polyester strings tend to lose the most tension and gut and Kevlar the least.*

more you stretch them (i.e., they stretch less for each additional pound of tension). String tension is obviously an important factor in feel and performance. A typical tension is 60 pounds (27 kilograms). Fifty pounds (23 kilograms) is low and 70 pounds (32 kilograms) is high. Some players are fussy about this and others are not, and some players can tell the difference and others cannot. (We will discuss this more in "Player Perceptiveness to String Tension.") The important point to keep in mind is that restringing at the same string tension as last time will only produce the same stringbed stiffness if you are using the same racquet, string model, and same gauge. Furthermore, it may even depend on the stringer's technique, the type of stringing machine, and the temperature in the shop.

But stringbed stiffness depends on even more than that. Many players don't realize that when you say "string it at 60 pounds" that you never get a racquet at 60 pounds. Even if a racquet stringer is very careful and pulls every string at exactly the same tension, by the time he finishes the last string, the first one will have dropped in tension. Not only that, every string will be at a different tension because the frame keeps changing its dimensions slightly every time a new string is added. It is common to find that the cross strings (the short ones) are 5 to 10 pounds lower in tension than the main strings (the long ones) after the job is finished. That's because the frame gets narrower and longer as each new cross string is added, so the mains get stretched further and the crosses keep getting shorter. Also, when pulling tension on the crosses, there is a lot of friction in the weaves between mains and crosses, so when the stringing machine thinks it has pulled to 60 pounds, some of that tension resistance is due to friction, not to string stretching, so the actual tension in the string ends up less than the 60 pounds of resistance recorded by the stringing machine.

And then, each string material starts losing tension at rates that are characteristic for each material. Most strings lose 5 to 10 pounds in tension in the first half hour (see Figure 2.6). Polyester strings lose tension faster than nylon strings. If you don't believe that, hang a heavy weight on the end of a nylon string and watch what happens. The string will stretch by about one-half inch when you first add the weight. Then, before your very eyes, it will stretch a bit further over the next few minutes. Come back the next day, and it will have stretched as much again, even though the weight and, hence, the tension, have stayed exactly the same. This process is called "creep." In a racquet the string stays at exactly the same length forever, but the tension keeps dropping.

By the time the stringing is finished, no strings will be at the requested tension, each will be at a different tension from each other, and the tension of every string will continually decrease. But each of these things add up in a predictable way so that a good stringer will give you a racquet at the same stringbed stiffness every time. And if he has the proper tools, he will measure and write on a sticker attached to the racquet what the stringbed stiffness is when you pick it up. Then, you should periodically bring the racquet in to retest the stringbed stiffness. When it has decreased by 20 percent, it is time for a restring. Don't wait until your strings break. By then, it's too late—you have already lost many more points than you had to, cussed too many times, and generally felt unfulfilled and unsatisfied with your game.

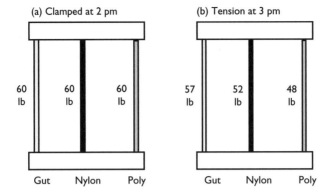

Figure 2.6 *Strings lose tension continuously over time. The loss is quickest in the first half-hour (actually the first 10 seconds), but it slows down and "stabilizes," except for a continuous creep that will diminish tension by several pounds over a couple of months.*

EFFECT OF STRING PATTERN ON STRINGBED STIFFNESS

An open pattern, 14 mains and 16 crosses, for example, will be less stiff than a closed pattern like 18 mains and 20 crosses, assuming the tension in each string is the same. Fewer strings resisting the ball impact will naturally stretch farther and thus be softer. Because the stringbed is softer, the total impact force on the strings will be less. This means the force on the ball is less, so in order to slow the ball down and reverse its direction, the force must act for a longer time. Also, because there are fewer strings, even though the total force on the strings will be less, the force on each will be greater and they will stretch more.

EFFECT OF HEADSIZE AND
STRINGBED SUSPENSION SYSTEM ON STRINGBED STIFFNESS

With larger headsize comes longer strings. At the same tension, longer strings are softer than shorter strings. For example, if a large head and a small head racquet are each strung at 60 pounds, the strings will feel stiffer in the small head and softer in the large head. A 60-pound string 10 feet long is very easy to push sideways, but if it is only one inch long, it will be very difficult to push sideways. Larger headsize doesn't necessarily mean the stringbed will be softer. That is because the recommended stringing tension of larger racquets is made higher in order to make the stringbed comparably as stiff as a smaller

Match Point Box 2.1

Rise in String Tension During a Shot

When a string is installed in a racquet, it needs to be stretched to arrive at the desired tension. Nylon strings need to be stretched by about 10 percent, gut to about 7 percent, and polyester strings, being stiffer, need to be stretched by only about three or four percent. By contrast, a steel string would stretch by only about 0.2 percent at the same tension. Steel is OK in a guitar or a piano because it doesn't need to stretch any farther when it is used. Tennis strings need to stretch farther every time they are used to hit a ball, otherwise they would feel too stiff and would

tend to cut the ball to pieces. The tension in a nylon string rises by about 30 pounds during each impact with a ball (for a hard hit) before it drops back to its normal value after the ball leaves the strings. It rises by about 20 pounds with natural gut, about 40 pounds with polyester, and about 60 pounds with Kevlar. Actually, the tension drops back to a slightly lower value than normal after every shot. After a few hundred shots the tension will be one or two pounds lower as a result of microscopic damage to the string.

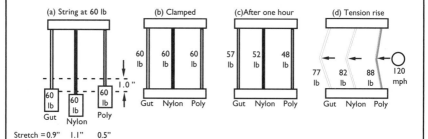

Figure 2.7 *Nylon stretches the most during stringing at 60 pounds, then gut, then polyester (a). All three materials are clamped at the same tension (b). After an hour gut is at the highest tension, then nylon, and then poly (c). So far it would seem that gut is a fairly stiff string—it is the second stiffest to pull to tension, and it is now at the highest tension. But, when you hit the strings with a force of a 120 mph serve, the strings will rise in tension (d). Poly will increase the most, nylon second, and gut the least. So, even though gut starts at the highest tension, it ends up at the lowest tension, and vice versa for poly. Gut stretches the most, gains the least tension, and is the softest material at all tensions typical for hitting a tennis ball.*

racquet of the same model. As a general rule, if you increase or decrease the tension by the same percentage difference as exists in different length strings, then the stringbed will have the same stiffness.

Two racquets with the same headsize and same dimensions can have different "effective" length strings, however. The effective length of string refers to where and how the string is actually anchored at the frame. Where the string is anchored combined with how it is anchored comprise the stringbed support system. In a frame with traditional grommets, which stick out from the inside edge of the frame into the string area, the anchor (where the strings bend) is at the end of the grommet. Racquets without grommets or with very large grommet holes (allowing free string movement and deformation) are anchored at the outside of the frame, giving the strings an extra length over which to bend and stretch.

Some racquets even have elevated, cushioned nubs on the outside of the frame that may further increase the effective string length, depending on the grommets and string hole size. And because these elevations are cushioned, they also decrease the combined material stiffness of the string and string support system. Decreased material stiffness combined with a "softer length" makes for a softer stringbed.

STRINGBED STIFFNESS SUMMARY

When it comes to stringbed technologies, everything can be described by the effect on the stringbed stiffness. Table 2.2 shows these effects.

Each of these factors combine to affect the overall stringbed stiffness. In a given racquet, you can adjust string material, gauge, and tension. If you are choosing a new racquet, you must consider all these factors. If you have become accustomed to one string and tension in one racquet, you may have to change both in a new racquet to duplicate the stringbed feel that you like. But then again, if the new racquet is stiffer or heavier, it may be more powerful than your old racquet, and you may have to change the stringbed characteristics simply to get the correct performance (speed, spin, and location of shots) as opposed to the desired feel. Table 2.3 summarizes the affect of the stringbed on performance.

Table 2.2 Effect of String Features on Stringbed Stiffness

String Description	Effect on Stringbed Stiffness
Long/short strings	Softer/stiffer
Thin/thick gauge strings*	Softer/stiffer
Open/closed string pattern	Softer/stiffer
Loose/tight string tension	Softer/stiffer
Soft/stiff string material	Softer/stiffer
Big/small grommet/string holes (support system)	Softer/stiffer

About half of all thin strings are stiffer than thick versions of the same string. The reason is that the stress (tension per square inch) on the thin string is larger and that the stiffness of most strings increases quickly when the stress increases above a certain value. A thin string will generally stretch further than a thick string when it is strung at 60 pounds, but it often stretches less than a thick string when the tension rises above 60 pounds during a shot.

Table 2.3 Effect of String Stiffness on Performance

Stringbed Property	Power	Control	Shock & Vibration	Spin	Rebound Angle
Soft	More	Less	Less	Same	Higher
Stiff	Less	More	More	Same	Lower

TENSION AND PERFORMANCE

Because most players simply ask for the same string as before when they restring, the tension is the focus of most player's stringing decisions. Players generally decide on a string due to cost, durability, performance, and the stringer's advice. But whatever the reason, they tend to stay with the same string time and again. Consequently, the only variable they fiddle with is tension. They do so for various real and imagined benefits concerning power, spin, control, and feel. We will examine the effects of tension on these, all the while remembering that all we are doing when we change tension is to change stringbed stiffness and the consequent results of doing so.

TENSION AND POWER

Experiments with strings in the lab have shown that when a non-deformable hammer strikes any string at almost any tension, each string takes in the same amount of energy and gives about 95 percent of this back. Therefore the hammer is ejected at the same speed for every string. The differences are that stiffer (whether by material, tension, or both) strings will stretch less and exert a higher force on the hammer, but do so for a shorter period of time (shorter dwell time). The higher force for less time ejects the hammer at the same speed as do the softer strings exerting a lesser force for a longer time.

Nothing changes in the string's dynamics when you hit the strings with a ball instead of a hammer. The strings still give back almost all of the energy that goes into them, but the amount of energy the string actually receives will depend on how much of the available energy goes into compressing the ball instead. Just as we know from string tests how much energy the strings give back, we know from similar ball tests that a ball gives back only 55 percent of the energy that goes into it. Energy is divided depending on the relative stiffness of two colliding objects—more energy going into the softer object. For the hammer and string, the hammer is so much stiffer than the string that all the energy of the collision goes into stretching the strings (the hammer doesn't deform). But the ball and the stringbed are about the same stiffness as each other (the ball compresses the same amount that the stringbed deflects). So they each will get about half the energy, whereupon the ball loses 45 percent of its share, and the strings lose their five percent. If you change the stringbed stiffness by raising tension or changing to a stiffer material, then the stringbed will be stiffer than the ball and will not deflect as much, and the ball will compress more. More energy is directed into the ball, of which it obligingly loses 45 percent, and the ejection speed of the ball is less. The opposite happens if you lessen the stringbed stiffness by lowering tension. The strings will take a greater share of the impact energy, leaving less for the ball to lose.

How much extra ball velocity are we talking about? It's not as great as you would think, given the folklore on the subject and player's anecdotal reports. The old adage "string loose for power, tight for control" is true, just not to the extent that most people think (i.e., looser strings will not change power by 20 percent, 10 percent, or even 5 percent).

If you drop string tension by 10 pounds, the percentage gain in ball velocity will be less than two percent, or about 1.2 mph on a 60 mph groundstroke.

That is certainly not significant enough that you can see the difference in ball speed leaving your racquet or during its flight. But it can add several inches to the depth of your shot, which is significant depending on your usual consistency level and when viewed over the long-term of an entire match. But at the same time, a few inches is probably easily and automatically adapted to by the player altering swing speed by 1.2 mph.

At low string tension the ball lands deeper for three reasons. First, it actually is traveling a bit faster, so it will travel farther. Second, because the ball stays on the racquet longer with looser strings, the player will swing through a larger vertical arc during this time, and the ball will, therefore, take off at a higher angle and travel farther.

The third reason is more complicated. When the ball hits a soft stringbed at an oblique angle, it plows deeply into the strings digging itself a hole, and it thus encounters a small "hill" in front of it as it slides across the stringbed. This hill slows the ball more than would occur on a stiffer stringbed. In addition, there is more string movement on looser strings, so as the ball plows along, it is also pushing the strings ahead of it parallel to the string plane and using up energy doing so. This slows the ball even more. As a result, the ball slows more in a direction parallel to the strings than it does for a stiffer stringbed. This combined with the fact that the ball will rebound faster perpendicular to the strings with lower tension make the rebound angle off the strings steeper (closer to the perpendicular to the strings) with softer stringbeds. This sounds like it should make the ball land shorter, not longer, because the take off angle is not as steep. This is true if the ball hits a stationary racquet, but when the racquet is moving, it is not. Figure 2.8 shows the ball incident on tight and loose strings. The rebound is closer to the perpendicular for the loose strings. Now, if we add the speed and direction of the racquet to the rebound speed and direction, the launch angle for the loose strings is higher to the court, and the ball will therefore fly longer. This third reason for longer balls with looser tensions may be the most important. An alternative explanation of this effect is shown in Figure 3.8.

The increased depth with a lower tension is due to both an increased launch speed and angle, the latter being caused by both longer time on the strings and by a steeper rebound from the strings. Hitting the ball one degree higher will make the ball land four or five feet farther. If the ball is hit one mile per hour faster, it will land about one foot farther.

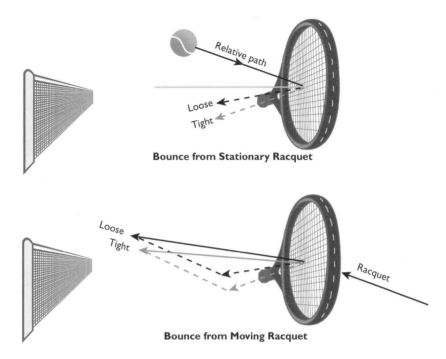

Bounce from Stationary Racquet

Bounce from Moving Racquet

Figure 2.8 *Loose strings cause the ball to rebound closer to the perpendicular to the string face. When you you add the speed and direction of the racquet to that rebound, the end result is a higher launch angle to the court, and thus the ball will travel longer. Chapter 3 will explain more about making this kind of "relative path" drawing.*

If the power difference is small at best and we can't actually see the speed difference during the hit, but only infer it by where the ball lands, and if the increased depth is due to speed and angle, perhaps the old adage should be revised to "string loose for depth and tight for safety."

TENSION LOSS AND GOING "DEAD"

When a string loses tension, it becomes softer. That is all that changes in a string. It does not lose power, resiliency, or go "dead" in any quantitative way. It simply becomes less stiff, and thus feels "different" to the player. A string doesn't lose resiliency. It is 100 percent resilient at all times, meaning that it returns to its pre-impact length every time. If it didn't, your strings would start to sag in the middle. Nor does a string lose elasticity. Technically, resiliency and elasticity are the same thing, but in common usage elasticity commonly refers to how much a string stretches. An old string used for many years will stretch less than when it was new, but it will still return 95 percent of its elastic stretch energy when struck by a ball. Likewise, when a string loses tension and, according to some players, goes "dead," it doesn't lose power or energy return, as the term would seem to imply. The string power is the same (if not more). We've seen that as tension declines, the string actually takes in, and thus gives back, more energy (which translates to ball velocity). So tension loss does not equal "dead" in terms of "power" (ball velocity), but in terms of diminished force of impact, shock, and feedback—in other words, in terms of "feel." Consistency of feel is very important. That is why you shouldn't leave your racquet in the car on a hot day—because heat accelerates tension loss, and, no, you can't get it back by sticking it in the refrigerator.

TENSION LOSS AND FEEL

The effect of tension loss on what you feel depends on several factors: the stiffness to begin with, the stiffness that feels best to you, your sensitivity to change, and how you interpret what you feel at a given stringbed stiffness compared to another.

You don't get the same "punch" when you hit the ball with diminished tension. The ball may go faster and farther, but it feels like less oomph. And because you have actually lost "control" as witnessed by the ball going farther (i.e., not where you are aiming), you may back off your stroke speed, which lessens the feel of impact oomph even more. So you haven't lost power, but you have lost the feel of providing the power, being in control, and getting feedback confirmation from the racquet punch. In essence, you have lost shock, not power. The impact doesn't shock you as much. Not as much shock is not as much "feedback." So, in one sense, when you choose a string, you are choosing the level of shock that feels good or proper to you. (However, "feeling good" doesn't mean that the level of shock that you like is good for you.)

No matter how you interpret the change in feel as tension goes down, the fact is that the feel does change. Strings do stabilize with time, and the rate of loss continually slows down. Consequently, a relatively "fast changing" string may still be slow enough to stay within your "feel range" for an acceptable amount of playing time. That will depend on your sensitivity and response to change.

Nonetheless, a rule of thumb does apply. Any strings at the same stiffness value should feel close to the same in the same racquet for a certain amount of time, no matter what amount of tension loss was required to arrive at that stiffness. The amount of tension loss is irrelevant as long at the resulting stiffness feels good to you. So, tension loss is not in itself a necessarily good or bad thing.

But, if you are unhappy with how long your string maintains its feel character-istics, then try a string of the same stiffness but that loses less tension over time.

TENSION LOSS AND CONTROL

Losing tension affects control (or the feel of control) in four ways. First, it may be that the lower tension results in more energy return to the ball from the strings, and the ball will travel farther with the same swing. Secondly, a lower tension will result in a longer dwell time. If you swing at the same speed, then the ball will stay on the strings through a longer part of the arc of your swing, both vertically and horizontally. The angle of your shot will therefore be affect-ed in both directions. And third, if you hit off center, the ball will twist the rac-quet for a longer time and affect the launch angle. And the fourth reason is the same as we explained in the Tension and Power section—the steeper rebound angle phenomenon with lower tension.

Sometimes players describe this as a "trampoline effect," or by saying that the "ball flies all over the place," or "I'm spraying my shots." The answer? Make the stringbed stiffer by increasing tension or choosing a stiffer string.

TENSION LOSS AND SOUND

The importance of the sound of impact is demonstrated by one very striking fact: about half of all players can't play without a string dampener, and the other half can't play with one. The auditory cue, or lack thereof, is absolutely necessary to all players in terms of feedback as to the quality of their shot. Some like to hear the "twing" and others find it off-putting.

Losing tension changes the sound of the impact. The pitch is lower. You can go from a "twing" to a "twang." "Twings" sound more responsive, elastic, and powerful than "twangs"—if that is what you are used to, anyway. This twang-ing will affect the psychology of your play. The secret is to tune your strings. Stiffness is the key factor in twings or twangs. The stiffer the string, the more the twing (or ping, if that is what you hear).

TENSION LOSS AND PRESTRETECHING

When a string is stretched and tied off at its stretched length, the tension starts dropping immediately. One could restore the tension by undoing the string and stretching and tying it again, in which case it would drop in tension again, but not by as much or as quickly the second time around. Some players there-

fore like to pre-stretch a string once or twice before installing it in their racquet. That way there is a smaller drop in tension per day than would otherwise
be the case. Alternatively, it is simpler to string the racquet at a higher tension
than desired in the first place. Prestretching thus slows the rate of tension loss,
but the string will also play stiffer at any given tension because some of the
stretch has been taken out of it.

TENSION AND SPIN

Another old adage says, "String tight for spin." Tests have shown that string
tension (or gauge, or material) has virtually no effect on spin. Yet players insist
they get more spin. What gives? The answer is probably two-fold.

First, because tighter strings produce less depth, the player swings harder to
get the depth back. A faster swing will then produce more spin. The second
explanation is based on an illusion of more spin. If the ball is leaving the racquet slower (i.e., assuming the player does not compensate with a faster
swing) with tight strings but with the same spin, the spin-to-speed ratio will
be greater, and the ball will bounce as if it has more spin. So, tight strings do
not in themselves cause more spin, but they might cause the player to create
more spin. The adage might thus be rewritten to read, "String tight if *you* want
to add more spin."

TENSION AND PLAYER PERCEPTIVENESS

Virtually every player assumes that he can tell the difference between different
tensions. Some claim to be able to identify a difference of a pound or two. Tests
have been performed that bring that claim into question. In a test of 41
advanced recreational players, only 11 (27 percent) could determine a difference of 11 pounds or less. In fact, 15 (37 percent) couldn't correctly identify
the difference even when the tension between two racquets varied by 22
pounds. A small number were able to discern a two-pound difference, however. Players were not allowed to touch the strings or vibrate them to guess tension, and each racquet had a vibration dampener to take away auditory cues.

Using earplugs to further dampen auditory cues lowered the success rates even
more. Players were only allowed four hits with each racquet, so the only data
the player was interpreting was feel, not an accumulated history of location of
ball placement that could be used to deduce string tension. Some players said
that they noticed a difference, but then incorrectly chose which racquet had a
higher tension.

The difficulty in deciphering the difference in tensions is because the ball speed and spin off the strings does not depend very much on the string tension. The speed and spin off the strings depends almost totally on how fast you swing the racquet. A ten pound change in string tension accounts for only one or two percent of the ball speed. So, if you are looking for changes in speed and spin to discern tension differences, you won't find much information upon which to guess.

However, string tension does have an effect on the force of the ball on the racquet so an experienced player should notice the way the strings feel by the force of the handle on his or her hands when striking a ball. It depends on how sensitive the player is to touch and feel.

These findings, of course, bring into question what players really feel or think they feel and how they describe what they feel. If they can't properly differentiate the feel of power, spin, and tension, what do they feel?

What is actually felt is the shock and vibration of the handle hitting the hand plus a push or pull on the arm. This sensation is made up of the rotation, translation, and bending of the racquet.

You don't actually feel the strings, but rather you feel how they alter the duration and amount of the thump and buzz of shock and vibration. The brain has to analyze this information and turn it into the vocabulary of "feel." As such, it is an interpretation, not a raw feel. And there is not enough information in this impact feel alone to produce the rich vocabulary that players use to describe the sensation—crisp, dead, grabby, clean, springy—nor is there enough information to determine the amount of power or spin.

The natural conclusion is that players "experience" the string; they don't just feel it. This is a holistic experience that includes feel, sight, sound, intellectual interpretation based on the placement results of many shots, and how the player knowingly or unknowingly alters his stroke as a result of those shot results. The interpretation then becomes the lens through which a player describes his "feeling." And then, the player attributes the cause of this post-facto interpretively constructed "feeling" as a characteristic of the strings— "these strings have a lot of bite."

However, there is no denying that string materials, tensions, gauge, etc., alter the performance outcome of a racquet and the player. Future string research will help clarify these phenomena and help us talk about them, but in the meantime, we will simply have to interpret each other's string babble. After all, we all know what we mean…right?

DWELL TIME AND PERFORMANCE

Much is said by coaches and players about "keeping the ball on the strings." Coaches advise to follow-through the shot to keep the ball in contact with the strings for a longer time, thus, supposedly, giving the player more control, touch, and feel. Others say this will give you more power because it will allow the ball to trampoline more and give the strings more time to accelerate the ball. As we will see, dwell time is independent of anything you can do as a player during impact, but it can be affected by altering the stringbed stiffness, which in turn will affect each of these things.

DWELL TIME

A tennis ball bouncing off a tennis court spends about 0.004 seconds in contact with the court. It takes slightly longer to bounce off the strings, about 0.005 seconds, because the strings are softer than a court and take a little longer to stretch and return to their original shape (Figure 2.9). The lower the string tension, the longer the ball spends on the strings. Also, the softer the ball, the longer it stays on the strings.

The contact time for a given tension decreases slightly when a ball (or the racquet) is traveling at high speed, despite the fact the strings stretch even further in a high speed impact. If the strings stretch further, then it's because there is a bigger force on the strings and, hence, a bigger force on the ball. The bigger force on the ball, combined with the longer distance traveled at a faster speed, means that the time spent on the strings is almost the same regardless of how far the strings stretch. Think of it this way. Driving a car 60 miles at 60 mph takes exactly the same time as driving a car 30 miles at 30 mph.

Some coaches recommend a long follow-through so that you can keep the ball on the strings a bit longer and direct the ball to where you want it to go. The advice is good, but the explanation is not. The ball spends about the same time on the strings regardless of the path or speed of the racquet. It's not like you are pushing the ball along a track for a few seconds or more. The ball hits the strings, rebounds, and leaves the racquet behind before you can do anything about it. By the time you finish your follow-through, the ball will have already landed on the other side of the court.

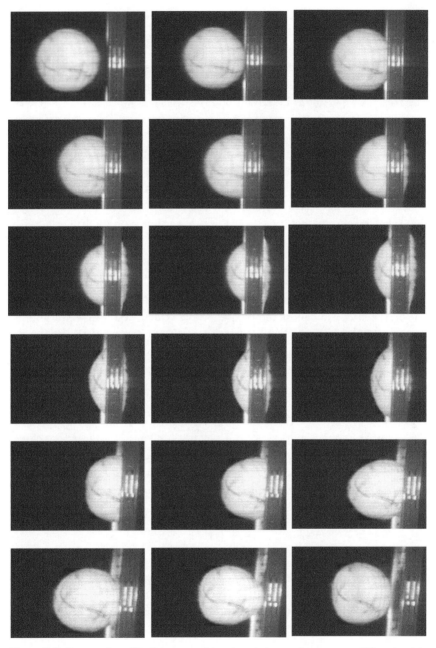

Figure 2.9 *Time series of ball impact with a head-clamped racquet at 90 mph with no spin at a 90-degree angle. Filmed at 2,400 frames/second (12 frames = 5 ms.) (Courtesy of the University of Sheffield, England and the International Tennis Federation.)*

The ball doesn't instantly come off the strings or the court; it stays there long enough to slide about two to four inches, depending on its speed and angle of incidence. That's why a ball leaves a skid mark on the court and why a ball sometimes clips the frame as it comes off the strings.

The reason dwell time is important with respect to control, even at the small variations that are typical, is not because it determines the time during which you can direct and control the shot, as some coaches maintain, but just the opposite—it determines the consequences of errors in the timing of your swing. At impact, the error has already occurred, and the dwell time will determine the consequences of that error. There is nothing you can do during impact; your fate is sealed at that point. It all has to do with dwell distance— the distance your racquet travels during contact time with the ball.

DWELL DISTANCE

When you hit a ball, over what distance does the ball remain on the strings? Is it about one inch, 10 inches, or maybe as many as 20 inches? Does it depend on the speed of the ball or the racquet? Does it depend on how you follow-through with the racquet head? You can work out the answer knowing the dwell time of the ball on the strings, which is about 0.005 seconds, regardless of what the racquet or the ball is doing. The dwell time can decrease to about 0.004 seconds if you hit the ball very hard or if the string tension is up around 70 pounds, but 0.005 seconds is more typical for a hand-held racquet.

For example, suppose you swing your racquet at 50 mph = 73 feet per second. At that speed, if you let it go, the racquet would travel almost the whole length of the court (78 feet) in one second. It sounds like a lot, but it is a typical racquet speed for a medium pace shot. A serve of 100 mph requires a racquet head speed of about 90 mph, depending on which part of the racquet we are talking about. The tip travels at about 95 mph in a 100 mph serve.

At 73 feet per second, the racquet travels a distance of 73 x 0.005 = 0.365 feet = 4.38 inches while the ball is on the strings. There is nothing you can do to change that apart from swinging the racquet faster or slower. In a fast serve the ball is on the strings for up to about nine inches, and for a slow drop shot, the ball is on the strings for only about one inch of the total distance traveled by the racquet head along its swing path. The follow-through has no effect on the ball. The follow-through is a consequence of what you do before you hit the ball, so it is an important part of the action, but a fancy flourish of the wrist at the end is purely for show.

DWELL ERROR

How does dwell distance contribute to dwell error—the distance range by which you can miss your target on the other side of the court? What if we increase the tension in our example above from 50 to 70 pounds, and suppose this drops the dwell time from 0.005 to 0.004 seconds. At a swing speed of 73 feet per second, the dwell distance will decrease from 4.38 inches to 3.5 inches. That is a difference of 0.88 inches. Does that make a difference on where the ball will land on the other side of the net? You bet.

If you were hitting from one baseline to the other, the distance is 78 feet. Now let's say the radius of the "circle" of your swing from a point near your shoulder to the impact point is about 40 inches. That means that the angle the racquet moves through for those extra 0.88 inches is about 1.2 degrees. That difference in launch angle at one baseline comes out to a 20-inch, left-to-right difference on the other baseline. So, for each stringbed, if you meet the ball at the exact same location in the arc of your swing and with the same swing speed, the difference in the side-to-side bounce location in your opponent's court will be almost two feet! You will have to adjust your stroke accordingly. But most players will only change tension 2-5 pounds, not 20. Within that range, few will notice a significant difference in the side-to-side dwell error unless they are extremely sensitive. However, a 1.2-degree error in the vertical launch angle has a much bigger effect than a 1.2 degree error in the horizontal launch angle (see "Trajectories" in Chapter 4). As a result, players should notice that they are overhitting the ball if the string tension drops by a few pounds.

DWELL TIME AND FORCE

The dwell time might be a millisecond longer on a soft stringbed. As a result, the force acting on a stiff stringbed is larger than on a soft stringbed. The racquet head is pushed backward by the impact, and the whole racquet rotates about an axis through the wrist. The rate of rotation is relatively slow for an impact on a soft stringbed, but the racquet will rotate farther during the impact. The hand absorbs the momentum of the racquet in much the same way as it does when you catch a ball. The shock of the impact will therefore be less using a racquet with soft strings.

Heavier racquets will have a longer dwell time. That's because the ball can't push the heavier racquet backwards as easily, so that energy will be directed into stretching the strings more.

Chapter Two

GENERAL RULES OF DWELL TIME

- Contact time decreases if the stiffness of the ball increases.
- Contact time decreases if the stiffness of the string plane increases
- Contact time increases if the mass of the ball increases.
- Contact time increases if the mass of the racquet increases.
- Contact time does not depend significantly on the speed of the ball or the racquet, although there is a slight decrease if there is a big increase in the speed of the ball or the speed of the racquet.
- Contact time for a bounce on a handheld racquet is about 4.5 ms near the racquet tip, about 5 ms in the middle of the strings and about 5.5 ms near the throat. That's because the tip is lighter than the throat.

Further Reading

H. Brody, R. Cross and C. Lindsey, The Physics and Technology of Tennis, Racquet Tech Publishing, Solana Beach, USA (2002).

H. Brody, Tennis Science for Tennis Players, University of Pennsylvania Press, 1987.

R. Cross, Materials and Tennis Strings, Chapter 8 in Materials in sports equipment, Ed. M. Jenkins, Woodhead, Cambridge, (2003).

R. Cross, Flexible beam analysis of the effects of string tension and frame stiffness on racket performance, Sports Engineering, 3, 111-122, (2000).

R. Cross, C. Lindsey and D. Andruczyk, Laboratory testing of tennis strings, Sports Engineering, 3, 219-230 (2000).

R. Bower and R. Cross, Player sensitivity to changes in string tension in a tennis racquet, Jnl. of Science and Medicine in Sport, 6, 120-131 (2003).

R. Bower and R. Cross, String tension effects on tennis ball rebound speed and accuracy during playing conditions, Journal of Sports Sciences, 23, 765-771 (2005).

Balls and Bounce

In the blink of an eye a bouncing ball slows, changes its spin, slides across and bites into the court and strings, squashes and stretches, and rebounds. The very nature of the game depends on this 5-millisecond sequence of events.

BALL BASICS

BALL HISTORY

Tennis balls were used many centuries ago in France when they were made from leather and filled with wool or cloth. Hollow rubber tennis balls were used for the first Wimbledon Championships in 1872, but by 1875 they were covered in white cloth stitched onto the ball because of their better playing characteristics. Almost nothing has changed since then, apart from the composition of the rubber and the cloth. If you remove the cloth from a modern tennis ball, you will have almost exactly the same 40-gram, 51-mm diameter rubber ball that was used for the 1872 Championships. In some respects the old rubber ball is easier to play with because it feels a lot lighter, but the bounce and flight through the air are a bit erratic. A 40-gram ball is not a whole lot lighter than a 57-gram ball, but it feels a whole lot lighter because a rubber ball without its cloth cover is much softer. The force on the strings, transmitted through the racquet to the arm, is therefore a lot smaller.

RULES ABOUT BALLS

There are more rules in the game of tennis about tennis balls than there are about tennis racquets, strings, or courts. You can play with a five-pound brass racquet strung with fencing wire on an uphill cow paddock according to the rules, but the ball must weigh more than 1.975 ounces (56 grams) and less than 2.095 ounces (59.4 grams), and its diameter must be more than two and one-half inches (63.5 millimeters) and less than two and five-eighths inches (66.7 mm), as determined by whether the ball can fit through holes of those diameters.

There are additional rules about how high a ball can bounce. Dropped from a height of 100 inches onto a concrete slab (or any other suitably hard and heavy surface), a tennis ball must bounce to a height between 53 and 58 inches (see Match Point Box 3.1 for a comparison of different balls). There are various ways that the manufacturers can achieve this, but the most common is to take a 40-gram rubber ball and glue onto it a 17-gram cloth cover, three millimeters thick, made from wool and nylon. Manufacturers have tried all sorts of cover materials, but a felted mix of wool and nylon works best in withstanding abrasion on all sorts of surfaces and in not fluffing up too much. Fluffing up can be a problem, not only in terms of aesthetic appearance and feel in the hand, but it slows the ball through the air. That is why professionals choose to serve with the least fluffy balls when they select two and toss others away.

Sometimes the rules concerning balls become a matter of interest to the public at large. For example, players and tennis commentators sometimes complain that balls used at the US Open are faster than balls used in other major tournaments. What they are presumably referring to is that they travel faster through the air. How is that possible? There are three possibilities. One is that the air in New York is thinner than the air anywhere else. That's unlikely. No matter where on earth you are, provided you are near sea level, one cubic meter of air weighs 1.21 kilograms, and one cubic foot of air weighs 1.21 ounces, not much less than a two-ounce tennis ball. At high altitude the air gets thinner, but New York is essentially at sea level.

Another possibility is that the balls used at the US Open are heavier than everywhere else. If players were hitting ping pong balls or shuttlecocks instead of tennis balls, it is unlikely that they would make it over the net. Light balls slow down faster than heavier balls through the air. However, the rules of tennis are very specific about ball weight. If the balls at the US Open were the maximum weight allowed, they would be slightly harder to hit than the lightest balls allowed. Given that heavy balls slow down less but come off the racquet at lower speed, it would be hard to pick any difference in terms of ball speed through the air.

Match Point Box 3.1

Ball Testing to Compare New and Old Balls

(a) Compression test method: Force is increased from zero to about 100 lb and then decreased to zero over about 30 seconds. An approved Type 2 ball must compress more than 0.195 inch and less than 0.235 inch (forward compression, x_F) when the force is increased from 4 to 22 lb. The return compression, x_R, when the force decreases back to 22 lb, is always larger because the ball takes time to recover its shape. The ball gets stiffer the more it is compressed, but the average stiffness is about 100 lb/in. because it takes about 100 lb to squash it slowly by one inch. When compressed very rapidly, the stiffness can increase 5 or 6 times before the wall starts to collapse.

(b) to *(d)* Results for 40 different new, slightly used, and old balls, tested at a temperature of about 68° F (20° C) as specified in the rules of tennis. Old pressurized balls are softer (they compress farther for the same force) and don't bounce as high as new balls because air leaks out over time. All modern, new balls are stiffer than pre-1960 balls. Type 1 new balls were also tested. Type 1 balls are commonly used on European and South American clay and are allowed to be stiffer than the Type 2 balls commonly used in the USA.

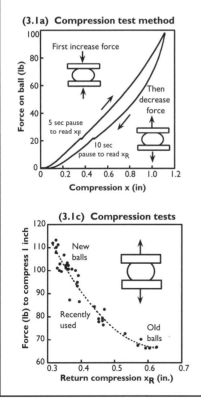

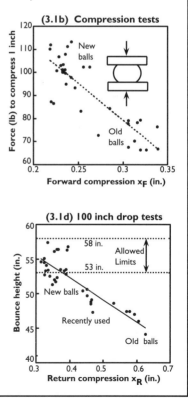

That leaves one possibility. The balls at the US Open might be smaller than other balls, or less fluffy. Air resistance is proportional to the cross-sectional area of a ball (including the fluff) and is 10 percent less on a 63.5 mm diameter ball than a 66.7 mm ball. It doesn't mean that the smaller ball will travel 10 percent faster than the larger ball. It means that the reduction in ball speed is about seven percent less. An average diameter ball served at 100 mph will slow down to about 74 mph by the time it lands on the court. That's a drop of 26 mph. The smallest ball allowed will slow down to about 75 mph, a drop of 25 mph. That's the same landing speed as an average ball served at 101 mph. So when people claim that the balls at the US Open are faster, they are claiming that they might be about one percent faster. And that's without actually measuring the speed or the diameter or the weight of the ball. It gets reported in the press because it makes a good story, but like many other stories, the facts sometimes get in the way.

A few years ago a rumor got started that baseballs in the USA were being juiced to go farther. The balls were indeed going farther because people were hitting them harder, but an extensive investigation revealed that the balls were exactly the same as they had been for the previous 20 years. Tennis balls have been the same for at least the last 20 years, at least within the tolerances allowed by the rules.

PRESSURIZED AND PRESSURELESS BALLS

There are two types of ball, but you can't tell the difference just by looking at them or squeezing or bouncing them. One is sold in a pressurized can, and one is sold in a cardboard box. Those sold in a can contain air at moderately high pressure. The can is also pressurized to help stop the air in the ball leaking out while it sits on the shelf. The air in the ball makes the ball stiffer, in the same way that air pumped into a balloon makes the balloon stiffer, or air in a basketball makes the basketball stiffer. Balls sold in a box are not pressurized, but the rubber wall is slightly thicker than usual to stiffen the ball. Pressureless balls last longer than pressurized balls (and cost more) because there is no excess air inside the ball to leak out. Pressureless balls tend to be more popular in Europe.

BALL BOUNCE OFF THE COURT

Tennis played on the red clay of Roland Garros at the French Open seems to be a different sport than tennis played on the Centre Court grass at

Wimbledon. The events, flow, and look of the game are completely different. And for good reason—the bounce of the ball is completely different on each surface, and it is the bounce that determines the game.

That five-millisecond bounce dictates everything, including shot selection, tactics, strategy, stroke mechanics, grips, and training. In a blink of an eye the ball's speed, spin, direction, height, and angle are changed. And these in turn dictate what kind of strokes and strategy a player adopts as he learns the game.

Though the ball is only in contact with the court for a brief moment, it has time to go through some or all of the following stages: slowing, spinning, sliding, biting, stretching, and squashing.

These events interact to produce a mind-boggling, if not ball-boggling, sequence of events that we shall explore. You will never look at the television broadcast's "HawkEye" or "Shot Spot" replay of a bounce the same way again. Those innocent-looking computer-generated skid marks are the forensic remnants of an incredible sequence of happenings that, until now, you simply thought of as "in" or "out."

FRICTION

Before we discuss the bounce off the court, we need to explain how friction works on everyday objects. We will then be in a better position to explain how friction can act in several different ways to slow down a bouncing ball and to change its spin. That's where all the action is. It's the most important part, but it's also the most complicated part and the one that has lead to the most arguments and misconceptions concerning the role of strings, strokes, and courts in generating ball spin and in causing the ball to "kick" when it bounces.

Friction plays such a dominant role in everything we do that we usually take it for granted. We only notice it when it's not there. It's the same with an injury. We normally take special notice of our arms and fingers and legs only when we injure them. Friction allows us to walk and run on a tennis court without slipping and sliding all over the place; it allows us to hold and swing a racquet without having it slip out of our hand; it holds all the strings in a racquet in place; it stops our shoelaces untying themselves and falling out of our shoes; it stops the net falling down; it holds screws and bolts in place; it allows us to hold a pen or pencil between our fingers, and so on.

There are three different situations where friction occurs, known as sliding friction, rolling friction, and static friction. You see these in action every day, and you see them all the time on a tennis court.

Sliding friction. Sliding friction results when one surface is sliding on another. Sliding friction acts to slow a ball while it is sliding on the court or on the strings. It also slows a player who slides into a shot on a slippery, sand-covered surface. Sliding friction acts in the opposite direction to the sliding motion and always slows that motion.

As we will see, sliding friction is the most important friction force in the bounce of a ball, and the factors that affect it are the speed and angle of incidence of the ball and the hardness or roughness of the court (or strings). Sliding friction does all the work on the tennis ball that we are concerned with—changing its speed and spin.

Rolling friction. Rolling friction is a much weaker force and acts when a ball is rolling on the court. Rolling friction is different because the surfaces in contact don't actually slide across each other. You can roll a ball easily from one end of the court to the other without it slowing much. But you can't easily slide a shoe or a racquet from one end of the court to the other because sliding friction will quickly slow them to a stop.

As prevalent as the rolling ball is on a tennis court, rolling friction is not evident in the bounce of a tennis ball. Instead, the rolling state is considered more as a transition point between the ball's sliding and biting stages during the bounce. This is so for the following reason: When a ball rolls, all points on the circumference are moving at the same speed, and the ball travels a distance equal to the circumference with every revolution of the ball. The circumference is about eight inches, so if the ball is rolling at 10 revolutions per second, it travels 80 inches per second, or about 4.6 mph. But as it rotates, the top of the ball is rotating at 4.6 mph to the right in the direction of motion, and the bottom of the ball is rotating at 4.6 mph opposite the direction of the ball. The bottom of the ball is, therefore, actually at rest.

Static friction. Static friction acts on an object when that object is at rest on a surface. For example, while you are walking, one foot comes to rest on the ground while the other moves through the air. The horizontal friction force on the foot on the ground is due to static friction. When you want to walk forward, you push backwards on the ground with your back foot, and the friction force from the ground pushes you forward. If you want to slow down, you push forward on the ground with your front foot, and the ground pushes you backwards. Provided the shoe and ground surfaces are not too slippery, your foot grips the ground while it is at rest on the ground, allowing you to push forward or backwards or sideways on the ground without sliding or slipping. If you push hard enough in the horizontal direction, your foot will eventually start to slide because there is only a certain amount of force that can be generated by static friction, after which your foot will lose its grip. Walking on ice or banana peels is more difficult because these are slippery surfaces, and the static friction force is relatively weak.

Static friction allows a shoe or ball to grip or "bite" a surface as if the shoe or ball were stuck down with sticky tape. The difference is that the stickiness of the "sticky tape" depends on how smooth or rough the surfaces are and how hard the two surfaces are pushed together. The grip force between a ball and the strings or the court is exactly the same type of friction force that acts between your hand and the handle of a racquet. The only difference is that you grip both sides of the handle while a ball grips on only one side. In both cases static friction acts to stop the contact surfaces sliding past each other, provided the surfaces are pushed firmly together.

As we will see, static friction plays a role in the bounce of the ball, but sliding friction plays a much more important role in changing the speed and spin of the ball.

BOUNCE FACTORS

The bounce of the ball depends on two forces: the force pushing the ball vertically off the surface (the "ground reaction" force) and that pushing against the forward motion of the ball at the court surface (friction). The action and effect of these two forces depends on a combination of factors: (1) the angle of incidence of the ball onto the court, (2) the speed (both vertical and horizontal to the surface) and spin of the incident ball, (3) the relative hardness or softness of the court surface, and (4) the smoothness or roughness of the court. These determine the rebound angle, speed, and spin of the ball off the court (or strings). We will refer to these as the four "bounce factors." The condition of the ball will also affect its bounce, but we will assume that we are talking about new balls in good condition, not old balls that have gone flat or lost a lot of fluff.

BOUNCE FACTOR #1: ANGLE OF INCIDENCE

The one thing we all remember from school is that when an object bounces off another stationary and immovable object, the angle of incidence equals the angle of reflection (see Figure 3.2). That statement is only true in two ideal situations: (1) when there is no energy loss and no friction, or (2) when the vertical and horizontal speeds of the ball decrease by the same fraction. For example, if the horizontal and vertical speeds both decrease by 20 percent, or if they both decrease by 30 percent, then the angle of reflection will be exactly equal to the angle of incidence. However, in most cases where a tennis ball bounces off the court, the vertical speed decreases by about 25 percent and the horizontal speed decreases by about 30 to 40 percent. After the bounce, the ball climbs vertically at a relatively fast rate compared with its reduced horizontal speed, so it bounces at a steeper angle than the incident angle. The angle of incidence is equal to the angle of reflection when light reflects off a mirror, but not for tennis balls bouncing off a tennis court. The bounce rule for tennis is that the angle of reflection is almost always greater than the angle of incidence. The only exception is when the incident ball lands with a lot of topspin, which we consider later.

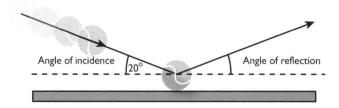

Figure 3.2 *If the angle of incidence is 20 degrees, the angle of reflection is usually greater than 20 degrees.*

The rebound angle depends on the angle of the incident ball, and it also depends on what happens to the ball in the horizontal and vertical directions during the bounce. If the ball comes in at a small angle, it will also bounce off the court at a small angle. If the incident ball approaches the court at a steep angle, the ball will bounce up at a steep angle. When a ball is hit with topspin, it tends to dive down onto the court at a steeper angle. Hence it will tend to bounce up at a steep angle. Each of these things happen because, when a ball hits the court, a vertical force pushes the ball up and a horizontal force acts to slow the ball and change its spin.

BOUNCE FACTOR #2: INCIDENT SPEED AND SPIN

A ball loses about 25 percent of its speed while traveling through the air. For example, a ball served at 100 mph lands on the court at about 75 mph. The bounce slows the ball about one-third of its speed, so it is traveling around 50 mph after the bounce. Depending on the type of court and the angle of incidence, the ball might keep low or bounce high, and it might slow down a fraction or it might slow down a lot. Only rarely will the ball speed up after it bounces, as it sometimes does in a topspin lob.

Figure 3.3 shows a situation where the ball is traveling downward at an angle of 20 degrees onto the court at a speed of 100 feet per second (68.2 mph). If the sun were directly overhead, the shadow of the ball on the court would travel horizontally at 94 feet per second. The horizontal speed of the ball is therefore 94 feet per second. If the court were 94 feet long, and if air resistance didn't slow the ball, the ball would take 1.0 second to get from one end of the court to the other. Similarly, if the sun were on the horizon, the shadow of the ball on the fence at the back of the court would travel vertically at 34 feet per second. At that speed it takes 0.1 seconds to fall through a height of 3.4 feet onto the court.

Regardless of the speed, angle, and spin of the incident ball, the vertical speed of the ball after it bounces is about three-fourths of the vertical speed of the incident ball. That's because one of the rules of tennis says a tennis ball must bounce vertically at about three-fourths of its vertical drop speed. Consequently, the ball in Figure 3.3 will bounce with a vertical speed of about 0.75 x 34 = 25.5 feet per second. In other words, it will rise up to a height of

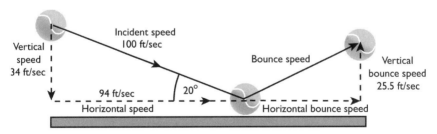

Figure 3.3 *The vertical and horizontal speed components of a bouncing ball before and after the bounce. On a bounce off the court the horizontal speed of the ball generally slows down more than the vertical speed. However, the effect of heavy topspin can create exceptions to that rule, especially on topspin lobs where the ball may actually speed up in the horizontal direction after the bounce.*

2.55 feet in 0.1 seconds. On some courts the ball will bounce slightly faster or slightly slower in the vertical direction. On a clay court, for example, the ball can dig a small hole in the clay, and it might then get deflected upward at a vertical speed of about 0.85 x 34 = 28.9 feet per second.

On most shots (except overheads and some serves and volleys in which you hit down into the court), the vertical speed of the ball toward the court is almost totally determined by gravity. Simply put, the ball drops from the maximum height attained in its trajectory. You don't usually hit the ball down onto the court; it falls into the court. The horizontal speed of the ball before the bounce has almost nothing to do with the vertical impact speed or how high it will bounce. However, the horizontal speed does affect the spin of the bouncing ball, which does have a small effect on bounce height.

The spin of the ball will also affect the vertical impact speed. Topspin creates an airflow force known as the Magnus force (see Figure 4.3, Chapter 4). This force pushes a topspin ball down during its flight through the air, creating more vertical speed and a steeper impact angle, and it pushes a backspin ball upward, thereby decreasing the angle of impact. Furthermore, a ball hit with topspin is likely to take off from the racquet at a higher angle and reach a higher apex in its trajectory, so it will drop from a greater height, gain more speed, and hit at a steeper angle. Topspin balls will, therefore, usually hit the court faster and steeper and bounce faster and higher in the vertical direction than will balls hit flat or with backspin.

BOUNCE FACTOR #3: HARDNESS OF COURT

The height of the bounce depends on the magnitude of the force pushing the ball off the court. This depends on the hardness of the court and the vertical impact speed of the ball. We have discussed the latter; let's now discuss the first.

When the ball impacts the court, it exerts a force on the court, and the court exerts an equal and opposite force on the ball. This force can be divided into two parts. Because the ball is landing at an angle, part of the force is pushing down into the court and part is pushing along its surface. So the court pushes back in the vertical and horizontal directions (Figure 3.4). That's why the ball bounces up and slows down horizontally.

The magnitude of the upward force on the ball, known as the "ground reaction force," is determined by the vertical incident speed of the ball and the relative

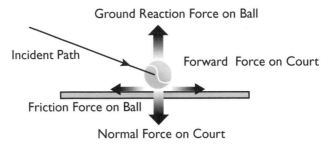

Figure 3.4 *The force of the ball on the court is equal and opposite the force of the court on the ball. The force on the ball has two component parts: one pushing upward, known as the ground reaction force, which causes the ball to bounce, and the other is the friction force, which resists the forward motion of the ball across the court and thus slows it down.*

hardness of the court and the ball. If the court is soft, energy will be lost deforming the court surface (or worse, if the ball lands in a pile of dirt, it won't bounce at all). The surface does not spring back fast enough or efficiently enough to aid the ball in its bounce, so that energy is "lost," and the ball won't bounce as high. Every surface tends to lose a characteristic amount of energy, which determines the vertical bounce speed (and thus height) for that court.

Some hard courts, such as those used at the US and Australian Open, are constructed with a layer of rubber under the top acrylic surface. The acrylic green paint is mixed with sand to control the surface friction on the ball while the rubber helps cushion the surface under foot. The vertical bounce height off these courts remains relatively high, despite the soft rubber cushion, because the ball doesn't compress the surface as much as it compresses grass. Hard courts are described as hard because they are much harder than the ball.

The ratio of the ball's vertical speed after the bounce to that before is known as the "coefficient of restitution" (COR). If the vertical speed after the bounce is faster on one court than another, the ball will bounce higher on that court. COR is about 0.75 for grass, 0.8 for hard courts, and 0.85 for clay courts. The effect of these differences is shown in Figure 3.5. The ball's vertical bounce will be highest and fastest on clay, lowest and slowest on grass.

COR is not constant, however. The efficiency of the bounce deteriorates at higher impact speeds, and COR will be less. Higher speeds cause more ball deformation, which causes energy loss. But, at the same time, as the ball deforms more, it gets stiffer and is harder to deform. These two effects work in opposite directions such that the net result is that a faster ball will always

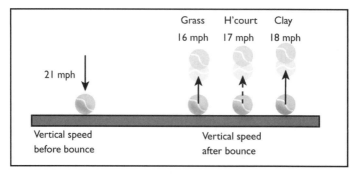

Figure 3.5 *The COR specifies the ratio of the vertical speed of the ball after the bounce to the vertical speed before the bounce. Courts with a higher COR will have a higher and faster bounce.*

bounce higher than a slower one, but it will not bounce higher in direct proportion to the speed increase, but something less. For example, if the COR is 0.75 for a low speed bounce, then it will be about 0.70 for a high-speed bounce.

That's it for the vertical part of the bounce. The real excitement happens in relation to the horizontal bounce—that part of the bounce that is most difficult to predict and that we associate with the power and heaviness of a shot.

BOUNCE FACTOR #4:
COURT SMOOTHNESS OR ROUGHNESS

For each of the three types of friction (sliding, rolling, and static), the magnitude of the friction force depends on two main factors. One is the smoothness or roughness of the two surfaces as measured by the coefficient of friction (COF), which is a number typically between about 0.1 (for a slippery surface) and about 0.9 (for a rough surface). The other main factor is the force acting at right angles to the surface (the "normal" force). The vertical speed of the incident ball and the court hardness determine the magnitude of this force pushing the ball and court together.

It is easier to see how surface roughness and the normal force affect the friction force by trying to pull a heavy block across a surface. Suppose you slide or drag a 10-pound block of wood across a horizontal surface. If the COF happens to be 0.5, then it would take a horizontal force of five pounds to slide that block of wood at constant speed. If the COF were 0.8, then you would need to increase the horizontal force to eight pounds to make the block slide at constant speed. However, if the block of wood were 100 pounds instead of 10 pounds, and if the COF were 0.5, then it would take a horizontal pull or push force of 50 pounds to slide the block at constant speed (Figure 3.6). If you tried to push that 100-pound block with a force less than 50 pounds, then the block wouldn't move at all because it would be stuck to the surface by static friction.

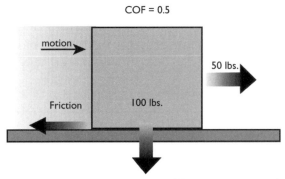

COF = 0.5

motion

50 lbs.

Friction

100 lbs.

Figure 3.6 *If the COF is 0.5 between a 100 lb block and the floor, it will take a horizontal force of 50 lb to move the block in a horizontal direction. It takes a vertical force of 100 lb to lift the block vertically.*

Players on a clay or sandy court usually slide to a stop as they approach the ball. In that case, friction between the shoes and the court acts to slow the player over a distance of perhaps one or two feet, and a slide mark is left on the court. The friction force is bigger on a heavy person than a light person (i.e., greater normal force), which is handy, otherwise a light person might stop too quickly and fall over, while a heavy person might slide all the way into the fence. The friction force doesn't depend on the contact area or the size of the shoes, and it doesn't depend on the sliding speed. The last two factors are probably not what you would expect, but experiments show that this is almost always the case. There are a few special exceptions, particularly regarding rubber, but the effect is not large. For example, wider tires can be used on cars to increase the friction, but we are not allowed to use wider tennis balls, and the outer surface is not rubber, so we needn't worry too much about that.

HORIZONTAL BOUNCE SPEED

The horizontal speed immediately after the bounce from the court depends primarily on the amount of sliding friction generated between the ball and the court and its duration and direction. Figure 3.7 shows a good example of the effects of friction for different courts on the horizontal speed of the ball.

If the ball is incident on the court at a low angle, around 20 degrees or less, which is typical of a fast first serve or a low, hard groundstroke, then the ball will slide throughout the bounce. In that case, the horizontal speed of the ball when it bounces will depend on whether the court is rough or smooth, and it also depends on the angle of incidence. The results in Figure 3.7 are typical for a medium pace serve. Serves at 100 mph or more are incident at around 12 degrees on the court, and they bounce faster mainly because they arrive faster, but also because the slowing down effect is weaker at smaller angles of incidence. The slowing down effect is weaker because the ball doesn't press as hard onto the court or squash as much as it does at higher angles of incidence.

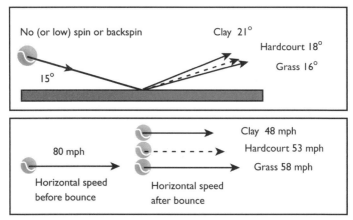

Figure 3.7 *Different court surfaces present more or less friction force to the ball, thus changing the horizontal speed and the direction of the bounce.*

When the ball is incident at angles greater than about 20 degrees (which is almost always the case for impacts on the strings where the angle is typically 70 or 80 degrees), the bottom of the ball slides to a complete stop during the bounce, and it then grips the court. If that happens, then the change in speed of the ball doesn't depend on the smoothness or roughness of the surface. In other words, under these conditions, a ball incident at any given angle and speed slows down by about the same amount on all court and string surfaces. There are two exceptions where the ball will slow even more. The first is for bounces on a clay court. Here the ball digs a groove in the court and has to push clay ahead of it. The force needed to push the clay, combined with the friction force on the bottom of the ball, results in a slower bounce than on any other court.

The second exception is that even if the ball bites the strings, it slows down more as it slides across the strings of a racquet if the strings are at low tension rather than high tension. This can be attributed to an effect similar to the effect on clay. That is, the ball digs a deeper "hole" into the strings at low tension than it does at high tension. The string plane does not remain flat while the ball is on the strings, but it deforms, and it tends to wrap itself around the ball. Therefore, the front of the ball encounters a small hill while it is sliding. The ball pushes against this hill rather than skimming over the surface, so it slows down more than that due to pure sliding friction (see Figure 3.8). At low string tension, the speed of the ball off the strings is slightly larger in a direction perpendicular to the strings and slightly lower in a direction parallel to the strings. The end result is that a ball bouncing off strings at low tension travels higher over the net and at slightly higher speed, so the ball will travel significantly farther before it lands. An interesting example of this is when a player breaks a string during a shot. The usual result is that the ball lands out past the baseline or hits the back fence.

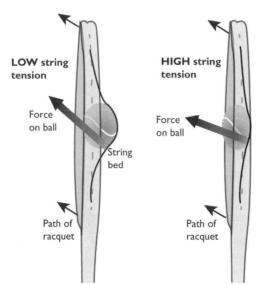

Figure 3.8 *Because the racquet is traveling upward and forward, the ball is projected upward and forward, but not at the same angle. The distorted shape of the string bed results in a greater upward force on the ball at low string tensions. In effect, the ball sits on a small ledge formed by curvature of the stringbed.*

The horizontal bounce speed also depends to some extent on whether the ball arrives without spin or with topspin or backspin, as we will see in the next section, especially when the angle of incidence is above 20 degrees.

EFFECTS OF FRICTION ON BALL SPIN

Figure 3.9 shows a ball in contact with a surface. We assume that it has just collided with the surface at an angle, so it has started to squash, and it is sliding along the surface. The force on the ball due to friction acts backwards on the bottom of the ball, in a direction parallel to the surface, so it acts to slow the bottom of the ball. The friction force doesn't act on the top of the ball, so the top of the ball will continue to move in a direction parallel to the surface at essentially the same speed as when the ball first landed. How can that be? If the bottom of the ball is slowing down, shouldn't the whole ball be slowing down? The answer is that the ball as a whole slows down, but the top doesn't slow down much at all. As a result, the ball comes off the court or the strings spinning rapidly. If the ball was spinning before it hit the court or the strings, then the spin will change during the bounce.

Suppose you are walking along and you trip on a step or a rock. Your foot comes to a stop, but your head keeps going at the same speed as it was going before you tripped. It's the same when a tennis ball hits the court or the strings

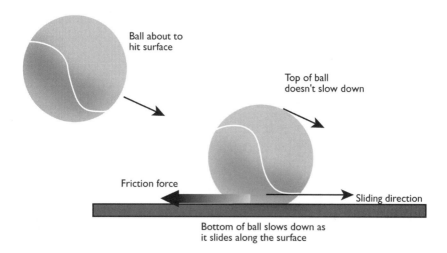

Ball about to hit surface

Top of ball doesn't slow down

Friction force

Sliding direction

Bottom of ball slows down as it slides along the surface

Figure 3.9 *The ball here starts spinning clockwise when it bounces due to the friction force on the bottom of the ball. The bottom slows down but the top keeps going.*

of your racquet. When you trip, you rotate forward. When a ball hits a surface, it starts rotating because the top of the ball is traveling faster than the bottom. The difference between a trip and a slide is that for a trip your foot comes to a complete stop instantly, but the bottom of a sliding ball takes a bit longer to come to a stop. On a slippery surface it takes a relatively long time for the bottom of the ball to slide to a complete stop. On a rough surface a sliding ball stops more quickly, but in either case, at the moment each ball stops sliding, it will have slowed and changed its spin by the same amount. In other words, if the bottom of the ball comes to a stop before the ball bounces, then the slipperiness or roughness of the surface will make no difference at all to how fast the ball rotates or spins when it bounces.

That's why many people have the wrong impression that more friction will generate more spin. It can, but it usually doesn't. The only way that the ball will have more spin when there is more friction is if the ball bounces before the bottom of the ball comes to a stop. For that to happen, the ball has to impact the surface at a small angle, as it does when you send down a fast first serve. The ball hits the court at an angle of about 12 degrees in a fast serve, in which case the ball speed and spin after the bounce do depend on the smoothness or roughness of the court. That's why fast courts are fast and slow courts are slow. But when you hit a ball with the strings of a racquet, the strings are nearly at right angles to the path of the ball, and the spin off the strings is the same regardless of whether the strings are rough or smooth, or whether they are closely spaced or widely spaced, or whether they are thin or thick.

Sliding to a stop. Figure 3.10 shows the situation in more detail. We see three balls sliding to the right on a horizontal surface at the same horizontal speed of 20 mph, but each is spinning at a different rotation speed. The first ball is not spinning at all, the second spins at 22 revolutions/second, and the third at 44 revolutions/second. Because the first ball is not spinning at all, the top, middle, and bottom parts of the ball are traveling to the right at 20 mph.

The second ball is spinning at 22 revolutions/second. The circumference of a tennis ball is 8.0 inches, so all points on the circumference spin around at 22 x 8 = 176 inches/second = 10 mph. Because the bottom of the ball is spinning backwards at 10 mph with respect to the middle, and the middle of the ball is moving forward at 20 mph, the bottom of the ball is actually traveling forward at 10 mph, and the top of the ball is moving forward at 30 mph.

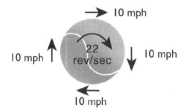

If a tennis ball spins at 22 rev/sec, then all points on the circumference rotate at 10 mph. At 44 rev/sec, the speed increases to 20 mph.

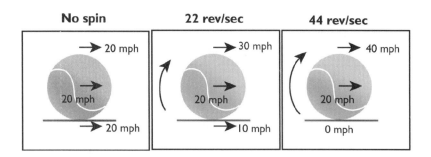

If a spinning tennis ball travels to the right at 20 mph, the speed at the top and bottom of the ball is 20 mph plus or minus the rotation speed at the circumference. The speed at the middle of the ball is 20 mph, since the rotation speed at the axis is zero.

Figure 3.10 *The sliding speed and direction at the bottom of the ball is the net sum of the ball's forward horizontal speed and the backward or forward spin speed at the bottom of the ball. Friction on the ball acts in a direction opposite to its sliding direction.*

The third ball is spinning at twice the speed of the second, so all points on the circumference are rotating at 20 mph. The middle of the ball is traveling at 20 mph while the bottom is moving backward at 20 mph with respect to the middle. The bottom of the ball is therefore not going anywhere because its total speed is zero. However, the top of the ball is moving forward at 20 + 20 = 40 mph. That's essentially what happens when the bottom of a ball comes to a stop after sliding along a surface. If the middle of the ball is traveling at 20 mph parallel to the surface while the bottom is at rest, then the ball will be spinning at 44 revolutions/sec, regardless of whether it came to a stop on a smooth surface or a rough surface.

If a ball starts sliding along a surface at 20 mph, without any rotation at the start, then friction will cause it to slow down to about 10 mph by the time the bottom of the ball comes to a stop. At that time, the top of the ball will be traveling at 20 mph, the middle will be traveling at 10 mph, the bottom is at rest, and the whole ball will be spinning at about 22 revolutions/second. If this happens, then the top of the ball doesn't slow down at all, the bottom comes to a complete stop, and the middle of the ball slows from 20 mph to 10 mph. The ball will then bounce off the surface traveling at 10 mph in the horizontal direction and spinning at 22 revolutions/second.

The biting phase of the bounce. When the bottom of the ball comes to rest relative to the surface, we say the ball is biting the surface. At this point, the bottom of the ball is truly stuck on the surface. The sliding friction force drops to zero and has no further effect on the speed or spin of the ball. Consequently, a ball that is spinning at 22 revolutions when the bottom of the ball comes to a stop will eventually bounce off the surface still spinning at 22 revolutions/second.

This phase of being stuck on the surface is difficult to visualize, but it happens in this way. When the bottom of the ball stops sliding, the top keeps moving forward, tending to pull the ball forward. At this point sliding friction gives way to static friction, which, as we have seen, works (up to a point) in a direction opposite the force trying to slide the surfaces across each other. In other words, static friction continues to act backward against the forces trying to pull the ball forward. During this tug-of-war, the bottom of the ball is stuck on the surface while the top, being elastic, continues to rotate and move forward, with the result that the ball twists and stretches out of shape. Eventually, this spinning and stretching top half of the ball will pull the rest of the ball forward and push the bottom of the ball backward, thus making the ball lose its grip. As a result, the bottom of the ball will suddenly start to slide backwards on the surface, opposite to the direction of the ball's overall motion and opposite from the direction it was sliding when it first began its bounce. Consequently, the friction force reverses direction and acts to push the ball forward. The additional backwards-directed static friction force immediately followed by a forward-directed sliding friction force combine such that the net effect of friction, after the bottom of the ball comes to rest, is close to zero. The result is that, contrary to everyday conversation, the bite phase has almost no effect at all on the spin of a tennis ball. Nearly all of the spin imparted to a tennis ball occurs during the sliding phase, and there is no, or very little, extra spin imparted to the ball after the court or the strings grip the gall. Grip action simply maintains the spin that was generated during the sliding part of the bounce, and it does not act to increase (or decrease) that spin by any significant amount. It does have a strong effect on a superball, and it can make a football bounce backward, but the effect on a tennis ball is much weaker because the ball is relatively slippery, and the grip is not as strong as it is on a superball or a football.

The duration of the slide phase depends on the incident ball spin. It might take 0.002 seconds for the bottom of the ball to slide to a stop if the ball is incident without spin. A ball incident with backspin will slide for a longer time because the bottom of the ball starts its slide at a higher speed due to its spin. It therefore takes longer to bring the bottom of the ball to a stop. If a ball is incident with topspin, the sliding speed at the bottom of the ball is reduced by the effect of spin, so the bottom of the ball will come to a stop sooner. A topspin ball will therefore slow less than a backspin ball, and it will also have a smaller change in its spin.

What are the consequences of this? It means that for two balls hitting the court at the same angle and speed, but one with topspin and the other with backspin, the topspin ball will come upon you faster and lower than a backspin ball. Lower because the ball travels farther horizontally while it rises upward through any given distance. For example, a ball incident with topspin might rise upward two feet off the court while it travels four feet horizontally. The same ball incident with backspin might travel only 3.5 feet horizontally while it rises upward by two feet (see Figure 3.11).

The topspin ball is more likely to reach a biting condition and therefore will slow less in the horizontal direction than the backspin ball. Depending on the incident angle, the horizontal speed will slow less than the vertical bounce speed. Consequently, a topspin ball is more likely to bounce at a shallower angle than the incident angle.

But this is completely opposite of what you experience on court. You know that the backspin ball will stay lower and seem to come to you faster. The answer is that topspin and backspin balls rarely will hit the court at the same angle. For a backspin and topspin groundstroke from the baseline to hit the same spot at the same angle would be virtually impossible. You could get them to hit the same spot, but the trajectories would be radically different. The topspin shot would land at a much steeper angle. A ball cannon can launch balls with topspin or backspin down onto the court at the same angle, but it won't be like this during normal play.

Nonetheless, our usual perception is wrong. Players and coaches are used to saying that backspin causes the ball to bounce lower and faster than topspin. Rather, it is the trajectory that causes such a bounce. The reality is that backspin actually causes the ball to slow more and bounce steeper than topspin, but backspin balls almost always take lower trajectories and thus lower bounces.

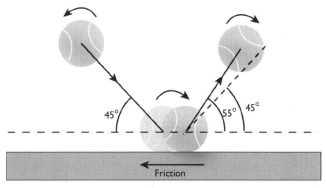

Incident with Backspin

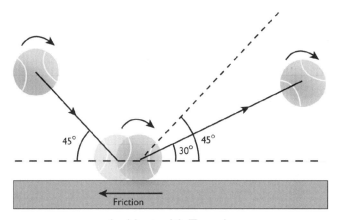

Incident with Topspin

Figure 3.11 *A backspin ball will slow horizontally more than a topspin ball hitting at the same angle and speed. Usually, and depending on the angle of incidence, the horizontal speed will slow more than the vertical speed. A back-spin ball will therefore bounce at a steeper angle than the incident angle. For a topspin ball the friction acts for a shorter time in the backward direction so the horizontal speed may not slow as much as the vertical speed, and the ball will bounce at an angle less than the incident angle.*

Balls that hit the court at less than 20 degrees will slide throughout the bounce, and sliding friction will determine how the ball bounces. Above 20 degrees, balls will bite the court at some point. The steeper the angle of incidence, the sooner that is likely to happen in the bounce.

What does this all mean? In general:

> • Lower angle impacts create less friction force, but it acts in the backward direction for a longer time; higher angle impacts create a greater friction force, but it acts in the backward direction for less time.
> • Friction acts longer in the backward direction on a ball with backspin than it does for a ball with topspin.
> • Low angle impacts are more likely to slide throughout the bounce; high angle impacts are more likely to start out sliding and then bite.
> • If a backspin ball and a topspin ball impact the court at the same angle, then the backspin ball will slow more and bounce at a steeper angle.

BALL BOUNCE OFF THE STRINGS

The mechanics of a bounce off the strings are similar to the bounce off the court in that the ball slides and bites just as it does on the court. Consequently, the same factors (i.e., angle of incidence, relative ball speed and spin, stringbed stiffness, and roughness of the string surface) influence the bounce, so everything discussed in reference to the court applies to strings also. However, there are four big differences that influence the bounce from the strings:

> 1. The strings are smoother than a court and faster than grass, so the COF is less.
> 2. The racquet is much lighter than the court, so it will recoil.
> 3. The racquet moves toward the ball, which changes the relative speed and angle of impact.
> 4. The strings are much softer than the court, so less energy will be lost in ball deformation.

Because the racquet is not as heavy as the court, that energy savings will more than be lost in racquet recoil at impact. As a result, the ball bounces at a lower speed off a hand-held racquet that is initially at rest than it does off a court. The player makes up for that by swinging the racquet, with the result that ball speed off the strings is usually faster than the speed off the court. Because the racquet and ball are both moving and the racquet face can be tilted forward or backward, the bounce off the strings is both more complicated and more interesting. So, we will next discuss the consequences of a moveable hitting surface. The main effects are on the angle of impact, the direction and duration of the sliding friction force, and the rebound direction and spin of the ball.

ANGLE OF IMPACT

It is not easy to visualize the angle of impact when the racquet and ball come at each other from different directions and speeds. The angle of the ball's incoming trajectory relative to the court before it bounces is easy to visualize. It is relatively easy to watch a bounce and say that the incident angle was 20, 40, 60, or 80 degrees to the court. But at what angle does the ball hit the strings? That is more difficult to determine.

First we must turn our visualization sideways because the strings are vertical. We still define the angle of incidence as the angle between the ball path and the surface, but now we have a vertical surface (Figure 3.12).

The racquet is seldom held still during impact. If the racquet is moving, the angle at which the ball hits the racquet depends on the relative speed and direction of the racquet and ball. It also depends on the angle of the racquet face to the vertical.

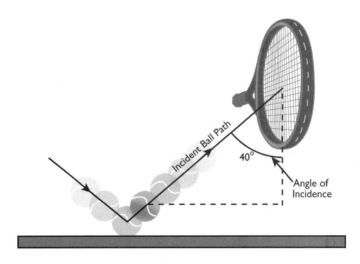

Figure 3.12 *Angle of incidence of ball bouncing from court hitting a stationary racquet. The angle of incidence in this case is 40 degrees, but what would it be if the racquet was approaching the ball at 50 mph?*

There is an easy method for sorting this all out. The method is what physicists call "changing the frame of reference." Essentially, the technique, as shown in Figure 3.13, converts the collision into what it would look like if the racquet were stationary and the ball were impacting it at the combined impact speed and angles of the two separate paths. Then, when we want to calculate the rebound angle (see "The Rebound Path" later in this chapter), we simply add back the racquet speed and direction to the bounce. The method consists of two steps:

1. Draw the paths of the ball and racquet at the desired angles, with arrowheads meeting at the impact point. Draw the length of the path lines proportionate to the speeds of the racquet and ball. For example, if the racquet speed is twice the ball speed, then that path line will be twice as long.

2. Draw another line from the beginning of the ball path to the beginning of the racquet path and put an arrowhead on the end. This line is labeled "relative path" in Figure 3.13 to indicate that it is the incident path of the ball relative to the racquet. The angle between the "relative path" and the string plane is the angle of incidence of the ball on the string plane. The length of the "relative path" line represents the speed of the ball relative to the racquet. By that we mean that if a ball approaches a racquet at 20 mph, and the racquet approaches the ball at 30 mph along the same line, then the speed of the ball relative to the racquet is 50 mph.

The three paths in Figure 3.13 are the same regardless of whether the ball is spinning or whether the racquet is tilted. The outgoing ball path will be different but not the incoming ball path or the racquet path.

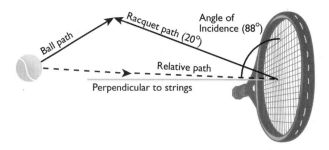

Figure 3.13 *Method for drawing relative ball path: (1) draw ball path, (2) draw racquet path, (3) draw resulting relative path by completing the triangle by connecting the starting points of the ball and racquet paths.*

The relative path of the ball is what you would see from the racquet's point of view. That is, it is what you would see if you were a bug sitting on the strings— a fuzzy yellow orb flying at you from outer space at the trajectory of the relative path. A familiar analogy would be if you are in a car driving along the road at 60 mph and you drop a tennis ball out the window. As far as you are concerned, the ball drops straight down and hits the road below (assuming, for simplicity, no air resistance). But someone standing on the side of the road sees the ball leave the window at 60 mph and land about 30 feet from where you dropped it. The horizontal speed of the ball relative to you is zero. Relative to the guy on the side of the road, the horizontal speed of the ball is 60 mph. You both see exactly the same thing, but the relative speeds and paths are different.

As you can see, the relative path result is sometimes surprising. In Figure 3.13, even though the racquet is rising to meet the ball, the impact is almost perpendicular (88 degrees) relative to the stringbed. If the racquet were to rise vertically at the same vertical speed as the ball, then the ball would remain level with the middle of the racquet until they collide. In that case the ball would approach the strings exactly at right angles. In terms of spin generation, the result would be exactly the same as if the racquet and the ball were both approaching each other along the same horizontal path. However, the speed and rebound angle off the strings will be different. The ball always passes higher over the net when the racquet rises up to meet the ball, compared to a case where the racquet head travels along a horizontal path at the same speed.

Now watch what happens if we increase the speed of the racquet. Figure 3.14 shows that increasing the speed, not the angle, of the racquet path changes the angle of incidence.

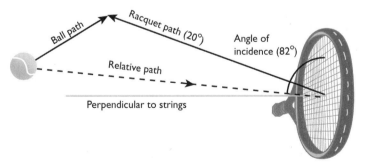

Figure 3.14 *Changing the speed of the racquet changes the angle of incidence. Here the ball is incident at a smaller angle than in Figure 3.13.*

The incident angle decreases from 88 to 82 degrees in this case, so the ball will rebound with more topspin. If a ball without spin is incident at right angles on the strings, it will also bounce without spin. Decreasing the angle of incidence here acts to generate more spin. The friction force drops, but it acts for a longer time when the angle of incidence decreases. Though the angle of incidence didn't change dramatically in this case, it nonetheless shows how changing the speed of the racquet changes the angle of incidence.

If we draw the ball going faster than the racquet (again keeping the angle of the ball and racquet paths the same), we get the result shown in Figure 3.15.

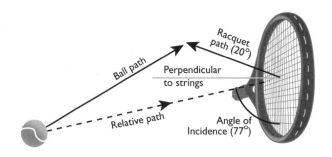

Figure 3.15 *Changing the speed of the ball changes the angle of incidence. Here the ball is rising up to meet the strings even though the ball and racquet path angles are the same as in Figure 3.13.*

Figure 3.15 shows that swinging slower than the ball speed will, in this case, cause the ball to rise onto the racquet, generating (in the absence of any incident spin) backspin on the outgoing ball. So, even if the racquet is swinging upward, you can still be imparting backspin to the outgoing ball. These kind of shots would tend to be more "blocking" type swings, perhaps like a half-volley or service return.

As shown in Figure 3.16, if you change the angle of your swing to a steeper path, for example, the angle of incidence will reduce and the ball will come off the strings with more topspin.

The general rule in Figures 3.13-3.16 is that if the ball rises faster than the racquet, then it rises up to meet the strings. If the racquet rises faster than the ball, then the ball falls down onto the strings.

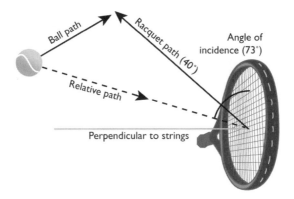

Figure 3.16 *Changing the angle of the racquet path changes the relative path of the ball (relative to the racquet). For a given relative speed, decreasing the angle of incidence always increases the amount of topspin of the outgoing ball.*

TILTING THE RACQUET HEAD

Not only does altering the speed and swing angle of the racquet affect the impact angle of the ball, but so also does tilting the racquet head forward or backward.

In general, on ascending relative ball paths, tilting the racquet face back will decrease the angle of incidence, and tilting it forward will increase it. For descending relative paths, it is just the opposite: tilting the face backward will increase the angle of incidence, and tilting it forward will decrease the angle of incidence. Figure 3.17 demonstrates these relationships.

Figure 3.17 *Changing the tilt of the racquet face alters the angle of incidence but not the relative path of the ball on the racquet. Tilting the racquet backward will increase the angle. Tilting the racquet forward will decrease the angle.*

THE BOUNCE PATH OFF THE STRINGS

The path of the ball and the path of the racquet both determine the angle of incidence on the strings, but what we are really interested in is where the ball goes *after* it comes off the strings. That is determined by the way the ball bounces off the strings. If you throw a ball at a stationary racquet, and if the ball is not spinning before it hits the strings, then (a) the angle of reflection off the strings is roughly equal to the angle of incidence, (b) the ball will come off the strings with topspin, and (c) the amount of topspin increases as the angle of incidence decreases and as the speed of the incident ball increases. The exact angle and spin can be determined by taking accurate measurements, but typically the ball bounces off the middle of the strings at about 40 percent of its incident speed, in directions both perpendicular and parallel to the strings. The bounce speed in a direction parallel to the strings also depends on the spin of the incident ball, but for the moment we will assume that the ball is not spinning when it hits the strings. Spinning balls are considered in Chapter 4.

There are three steps needed to work out the speed and angle of the ball when it bounces off a moving racquet. They are all shown in Figure 3.18. First, we need to work out the incident path of the ball relative to the racquet, as if the racquet were actually at rest. We have already seen how to do that by the examples in Figures 3.13 to 3.16. Figure 3.18a is just another example of the same thing for a case where the ball is hit on the rise by a racquet that is rising faster than the ball. For simplicity, we show a case where the racquet head is vertical rather than tilted. In that case, the ball is effectively falling down onto the racquet, as shown in Figure 3.18b. The ball will therefore bounce off the strings in a downward direction, as shown by the bounce path, at an angle approximately equal to the angle of incidence. However, this is the result for a racquet that is initially at rest. To get the corresponding result for a racquet that is actually swung at the ball, we have to add back the speed of the racquet, as shown in Figure 3.18c. We then find, in this case, that the ball rises upward off the strings and heads over the net, as shown by the outgoing ball path.

The method used to get the outgoing ball path is this:

1. Draw the bounce path arrow assuming the angle of incidence is equal to the angle of reflection, and draw it so that it is 0.4 times as long as the relative path. If the ball comes off the tip of the strings, draw the bounce path about 0.2 times as long because the ball bounces at a lower speed off the tip. If the ball strikes the strings with backspin, the bounce path will be closer to a line perpendicular to the strings. If the ball strikes the strings with topspin the angle of reflection will be less than the angle of incidence so the bounce path will be farther away from the line perpendicular to the strings.

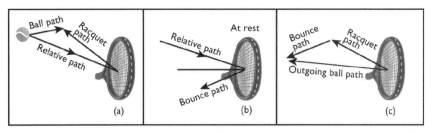

Figure 3.18 *The three steps needed to figure out the speed and angle of a ball hit by a moving racquet.*

2. Draw the bounce path arrow so its tail connects to the head of the racquet path arrow. That way, we add back the speed of the racquet to get the outgoing ball speed. The result is shown, in both magnitude and direction, by the arrow coming from the strings and ending at the tip of the bounce path. That is, the length of the outgoing ball path arrow represents the speed of the outgoing ball, and the direction of the arrow is the direction of the ball as it comes off the strings.

There are lots of possible ways to hit a ball by swinging a racquet. Most of them are included in Figure 3.19. The results in Figure 3.19 were obtained using the method we have just outlined. Looking at these various kinds of impacts allows us to make some generalizations about the rebound path.

The serve is the easiest to think about because the ball is suspended almost motionless in the air when you hit it. Figure 3.19A (a) shows the result of hitting the ball when the path of the racquet head is at right angles to the string plane. Provided you strike the ball near the middle of the strings, the ball comes off the strings traveling in the same direction as the racquet head. This is the simplest of all serve strokes, but there is no spin imparted to the ball.

Figure 3.19A (b), (c), and (d) show the effect of tilting the strings at some angle to the path of the racquet head. In these situations, the path of the ball after it comes off the strings is roughly half way between the direction of the original path of the racquet and a line drawn at right angles to the string plane. Tilting the racquet head is a common method of putting spin on the ball because the strings then slide across the back of the ball.

Figure 3.19B (a)-(h) shows eight different ways of hitting a forehand, backhand, or volley. The path of the ball is still roughly half way between the direction of the original path of the racquet and a line drawn at right angles to the

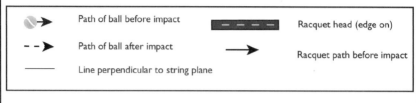

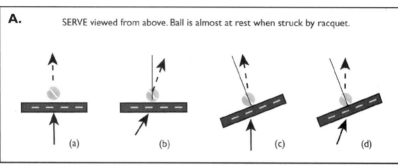

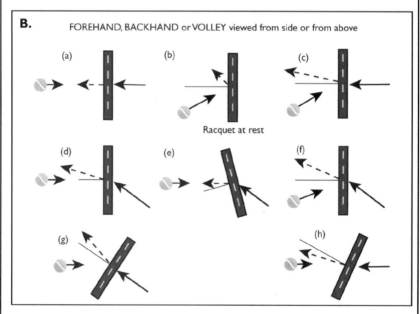

Figure 3.19 *The outgoing path of the ball is approximately half way between the racquet path and a line perpendicular to the racquet face (but not in cases such as (c) and (g) where the racquet path is along the perpendicular line and where the ball approaches at an angle).*

string plane, but there is an added complication. That is, the original path of the ball will also determine the bounce angle off the strings. If the ball is traveling along a line at right angles to the string plane before it is hit, as in (a) and (d), then there is no extra complication. The complication arises only if the ball is incident at an angle to the string plane. In that case, the outgoing path of the ball is deflected away from the incoming path because the ball tends to bounce off the strings as shown in (b). The situation is even further complicated if the ball is spinning as it travels toward the racquet.

The results in Figure 3.19B were calculated for a fixed racquet head speed and incoming ball speed. The angles tend to vary as the speeds are varied, but results (a) and (b) are independent of these speeds.

It is important to remember that the faster you swing the racquet, the closer will be the outgoing ball direction to the direction of travel of the racquet. Even pros have trouble with this. It is easy to hit a ball out over the sidelines, even though you might aim to hit the ball to land inside the sidelines, simply by swinging the racquet too slowly. In that case you get an effect something like that in (b) where the ball bounces off the strings at a large angle. The solution is shown in (c) where the outgoing ball path moves closer to the racquet path if the racquet is swung faster.

It is always safer to hit the ball straight back to your opponent, because the ball will travel back in that direction no matter how hard you hit it. If you try to change the direction of the ball, then the angle of the ball off the strings depends on how hard you hit it. It is therefore harder to judge the correct angle when hitting away from your opponent than hitting the ball straight back.

Further Reading

H. Brody, R. Cross and C. Lindsey, The Physics and Technology of Tennis, Racquet Tech Publishing, Solana Beach, USA (2002).

H. Brody, Tennis Science for Tennis Players, University of Pennsylvania Press, 1987.

R.C. Cross, The bounce of a ball, Am. J. Phys. 67, 222-227 (1999).

R.C. Cross, Dynamic properties of tennis balls, Sports Engineering 2, 23-33 (1999).

R. Cross, Grip-slip behaviour of a bouncing ball, Am. J. Phys. 70, 1093-1102, (2002).

R. Cross, Measurements of the horizontal and vertical speeds of tennis courts, Sports Engineering, 6, 95-111 (2003).

R. Cross, Bounce of a spinning ball near normal incidence, Am. J. Phys. (to be published late 2005).

Spin and Trajectory

Spin is the same off any string, whether it is soft or stiff,
sticky or rough, or thick or thin. Spin depends only on the speed of the
racquet head in a direction parallel to the string plane.

SPIN BASICS

The modern game of tennis at top levels is dominated by the amount of spin that players now impart to the ball. Spin plays an important role in all ball sports, for the same basic reasons. That is, the bounce angle off a surface is affected by the amount and direction of ball spin before the bounce, and the flight through the air is also affected by the amount and direction of ball spin.

A ball hit with topspin curves down onto the court more quickly than a ball hit without any spin, and it will hit the court at a steeper angle. As a result, the ball will bounce up higher. It may also bounce at a steeper angle, but it might even shoot forward at a lower angle. It depends on the angle of incidence and the amount of spin. Bounce height depends only on the vertical speed of the ball after the bounce. The bounce angle depends on both the vertical speed and the horizontal speed after the bounce.

The reason that players like hitting with topspin is that it makes it easier to hit the ball hard without the ball flying over the baseline. Consequently it is easier to pass a player at the net or to lob over his or her head. The modern game of singles tennis has evolved into one where most top players just run back and forth at the baseline, trying to keep the ball in play or waiting for an opportunity to hit a winner. In the good old days, players came to the net more often, particularly after the first serve. Older players blame the larger head size of modern racquets, which allows players to use more topspin because the ball is less likely to clip the frame. Old wood racquets were 9 inches wide and 27 inches long. It used to be standard practice to check the net height (36 inches in the middle) using two wood racquets. Professionals now use racquets that are typically 10 inches wide, which allows them to double or even quadruple the amount of topspin previously available with old wood racquets (Figures 4.7 and 4.10 explain how). That changed the nature of the game drastically during the 1970s and 1980s. Most commentators blamed (and still blame) the extra power of modern racquets, but racquet power has increased only a few percent. Racquet weight dropped with the switch from wood to graphite, but the extra stiffness of graphite made up for the loss in power of the lighter racquets. It was the wider frame that was responsible for the change in the game because players were able to swing their racquets faster when they were able to generate more topspin. There was a positive feedback effect here as well. More racquet head speed generated even more spin which allowed players to swing even faster. These days players almost launch themselves into orbit when they return the ball, hence the need to grunt or scream.

GENERATION OF SPIN

Topspin is generated whenever the ball bounces off the court, even if the ball hits the court with backspin. In order to change the amount and/or direction of that spin with your racquet, the ball has to be incident at an angle to the strings. That way the ball slides across the strings and then bounces off with spin due to the rotation generated while it was on the strings. From your own point of view, the ball doesn't approach the racquet when you hit it. Rather, your racquet approaches the ball. It's really the same thing seen from a different point of view. Similarly, the ball doesn't slide across the strings when you hit it. Your racquet slides across the back of the ball. Same thing really. However, it tells you how to generate topspin. That is, your racquet needs to slide up the back of the ball in order to make it spin. To do that, you need to swing the racquet head upward and forward so that the strings are approximately vertical when you hit the ball. You swing forward, so the ball goes toward the net, and upward, so the ball goes over the net and comes off the strings with topspin. In fact, the racquet slides for an inch or so, and then the strings grip or grab the ball, pulling the back of the ball up with the racquet until the strings shoot the ball out.

INFLUENCE OF INCIDENT ANGLE AND SPIN ON REBOUND SPIN

You create more or less spin by altering the speed, angle, and tilt of the racquet. Chapter 3 discussed how altering these variables changes the angle of incidence. When you change the angle of incidence, you are also affecting the magnitude, duration, and direction in which friction will work on the ball, which determines the spin of the ball. Friction force does not just act in a direction opposite that of the ball's motion, but it acts in the opposite direction to the *net* motion at the bottom of the ball in relation to the strings. "Net" direction means the result of adding the speed and direction of the ball's relative linear motion parallel to the strings and its spin (remember, "relative" motion means that we have determined the speed and path of the ball relative to the racquet, as described in Chapter 3).

Match Point Box 4.1

Effects of Spin on Bounce off the Strings

If you drop a ball vertically down onto the court without spin, the ball will bounce vertically up without spin. However, if you drop a spinning ball vertically down onto the court, the ball will bounce up at an angle with reduced spin. The bigger the spin, the bigger the angle. The same thing happens if you drop a spinning ball onto the strings of a racquet. That is, the ball bounces up at an angle. The same thing also happens if a spinning ball is traveling horizontally and strikes the strings when the string plane is vertical.

Following a serve, the ball spins rapidly as it bounces off the court. If you just block the serve or pat it back, the ball will tend to come off the strings at a high angle and may sail beyond the baseline. The problem is even worse if the player serves with topspin. The problem with a topspin serve

is that not only does the ball spin faster after it bounces, but the ball also dives into the court and bounces or kicks up steeply. As a result, a blocked or patted return of serve tends to fly up even higher.

To prevent skying the return of a high bouncing topspin serve, you can do two things. One is to hit the ball harder, and the other is to hit the ball downward instead of attempting to hit it horizontally or slightly up over the net. If you hit the ball harder, it will tend to go where you want it to go—that is, in the direction the racquet head is going. The vertical motion of the ball off the strings due to the incoming ball spin and the kick off the court is unchanged, but it becomes a smaller fraction of the total outgoing ball speed. As a result, the ball comes off the strings at a lower vertical angle.

A ball always has topspin relative to the court after it bounces. That court top-spin can look like either topspin or backspin to the racquet, depending on whether the ball is rising or falling relative to the racquet. If the racquet is actually rising up to meet the ball, then that is the same as the ball falling down to meet the racquet, in which case the ball is incident on the strings with backspin (Figure 4.1a). That is the usual situation when a player attempts to hit a topspin groundstroke. The problem for the player is that the spin of the ball has to be reversed, which requires a vigorous upward sweep of the racquet. Relative to the string plane, the ball will then be incident at a large angle away from the perpendicular, and it will bounce off the strings with topspin. If the racquet is not swung upward fast enough, then the ball is likely to bounce off the strings still spinning in the same direction, in which case it would come off the strings with backspin.

The task of returning the ball with backspin is much easier. In that case the player doesn't need to reverse the direction of spin and doesn't need to swing upwards at the ball. A horizontal swing of the racquet with the strings vertical is all that is needed. To get even more backspin, a player can hit down on the ball, which is equivalent to the ball rising up to meet the racquet. In that case, a ball coming off the court with topspin approaches the strings with topspin. Relative to the racquet, the ball will then bounce off the strings with topspin.

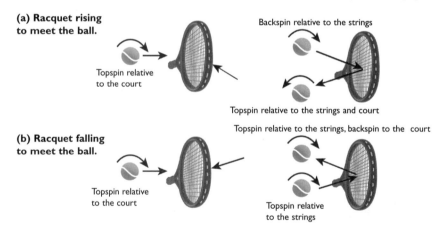

Figure 4.1 *(a) If the racquet is rising to meet a ball that is traveling horizontally, that is the same as the ball falling down to meet the racquet, so the ball approaches the strings with backspin relative to the strings. To return the ball with topspin, the spin of the ball needs to be reversed. (b) If the racquet is falling to meet the ball, that is the same as the ball rising up to meet the racquet, so the ball approaches the strings with topspin relative to the strings. To return the ball with backspin, the spin of the ball does not need to be reversed.*

Relative to the court, it comes off the strings with backspin (Figure 4.1b).

Types and Uses of Spin

A spinning ball follows a different path through the air and bounces different-ly than a ball without spin. Good players use spin to control the path of the ball as much as they use speed and angle. For example, the plan of attack when serving is to make sure your opponent has trouble returning your serve. There are five ways to do that. First, you direct the ball to the tee or the far corner so that he or she has trouble reaching it. Second, you serve the ball into the body so that your opponent has trouble getting out of its way. Third, you serve the ball fast so that he or she doesn't have time to prepare for a good return. Fourth, you swerve the ball through the air so it doesn't travel in a straight line. And fifth, you make the ball kick when it bounces. Depending on which way the ball is spinning, you can get it to kick left or right, up or down, forward or backwards, or any two or three of those. Attack plans four and five both involve spin. How and why does spin work to accomplish these goals?

Like anything else, a tennis ball has three main axes about which it can rotate. It can rotate about a vertical axis, a horizontal axis across the court, or a hori-zontal axis along the court. All three axes are at right angles to each other. A ball can spin about other axes as well, such as one that is tilted 30 degrees away from the vertical, but if we count every possible tilt angle, we would have an infinite number of axes to worry about. The three axes at right angles are called the principal axes of rotation. They are the only ones we need to consider because any other axis of rotation will generate some rotation about each of the three principal axes.

Topspin and backspin. If the axis is horizontal and across the court, then the ball can have topspin or backspin, depending on the direction of rotation (Figure 4.2). Logically, the opposite of "top" spin is "bottom" spin, but some-one decided years ago to call it "backspin." In topspin the top of the ball rotates away from the player who hit the ball or towards the player receiving the ball. Backspin is vice-versa.

Figure 4.2 shows the combined effect of spin on the flight of the ball and the bounce from the court. A ball hit over the net with topspin shoots forward when it lands. Hit with enough backspin, a ball can even bounce back over the net. Hit with sidespin, there is no deflection by the court at all, either forward or sideways. Hit with spiralspin, the ball will suddenly kick sideways when it hits the court.

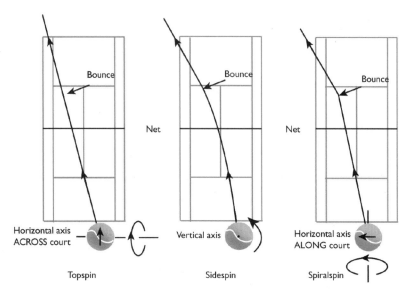

Bird's-eye view looking down on the ball and on the court.

Figure 4.2 *The three major axes and the spin around them. Topspin causes devia-
tions through the air and during the bounce. Topspin bounces high and also kicks forward. Sidespin causes deviation through the air, but there is no kick when it hits the
court. A ball spiralling like a football travels through the air in the same way as a
ball with no spin, but it kicks sideways when it bounces.*

Without spin, a ball travels over the net and lands on the other side because
gravity pulls it downward. With topspin there is an additional downward force,
called the Magnus force, caused by the change in airflow and a change in pressure on the ball (Figure 4.3). The air also exerts a backward force, known as a
drag force, which acts to slow the ball by about 25-30 percent from one end of
the court to the other. With backspin, the Magnus force acts vertically up on
the ball, and, hence, the ball tends to float or travel a longer distance before it
lands. Topspin allows a player to hit the ball a bit harder, and it will tend to
quickly drop or curve down onto the court without sailing over the baseline.

Sidespin. If the spin axis is vertical, then the Magnus force is horizontal and
the ball will curve to the left or the right through the air, depending on the
direction of rotation. It's the same effect as topspin or backspin if you view it
with your head tilted at 90 degrees. Gravity always acts down regardless of
which way the ball is spinning, while the Magnus force acts in a direction that
is perpendicular to both the spin axis and the direction of motion of the ball.
Spin about the vertical axis has been named "sidespin." The ball can spin

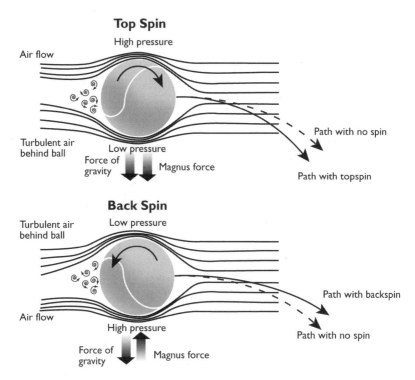

Figure 4.3 *The force on a ball due to its spin is called the Magnus force, and it is due to changes in air pressure around the ball caused by motion of the ball through the air.*

clockwise or counter-clockwise, but, in tennis, no one has given the two separate directions separate names. In golf, sidespin is either a hook or a slice, and players pay coaches to help them get rid of it.

Spiralspin. What if the ball is traveling from one end of the court to the other, and the ball is spinning around the third axis? In other words it is spinning like a football with the axis horizontal and pointing along the court? Then there is no Magnus force at all, and the ball does not get deflected by the air. However, there will be a sideways force on the ball when it lands, causing the ball to kick to the left or the right depending on the direction of spin. The usual situation is that when a player serves a ball so that it curves, say, to the left through the air, then it will straighten up when it bounces by kicking to the right. That's because the action of slicing the ball so it spins about a vertical axis also causes the ball to spin about a horizontal axis like a football. You can observe the action best if you stand behind a player when he or she is serving. That way you can see which way the racquet moves across the ball (up-down, left-right, front-back, or all three) to judge its spin, and you can then relate that spin to the path of the ball. The spin in this direction never got a name, being instead lumped in with sidespin. Of course this spin should have been called "sidespin" but since that has been taken (even if misnamed), we will call it "spiralspin." Clockwise spiral is "right spiral" and counter-clock-wise spiral is "left spiral."

The easiest way to hit a ball with spiralspin is to hit it underarm over the net, like a coach feeding balls to a beginner, with a right to left sideways chop of the racquet. The bigger the chop, the more spin on the ball and the bigger the sideways deflection when it lands. The same sort of thing happens when a player serves the ball or hits a groundstroke, unless it is a dead flat serve, where the racquet face is moving exactly perpendicular to the eventual path of the ball. If the racquet face is not perpendicular or is rising up to meet the ball or moving sideways across the ball, then the ball will acquire spin. It will gen-erally spin about all three axes simultaneously, but not all at the same speed. It's the job of the coach to teach the player how to control the spin so the ball swerves through the air and/or kicks upwards or sideways on command. Spiralspin is generated when the racquet is moving across the face of the ball (upward, downward or sideways) in such a way that the strings make contact with the ball at any point that is not exactly at the back of the ball—that is, not coincident with the spin axis. For example, when feeding a ball underarm, the strings contact the ball at a point underneath the back of the ball.

That gives us six ways to spin a ball: topspin, backspin, right sidespin, left sidespin, right spiralspin, and left spiralspin.

18 DIFFERENT WAYS TO HIT THE BALL

Each of the six different spins requires a different hitting action. Figure 4.4 shows six different hitting actions. In each case, the racquet must move toward the net so that the ball travels over the net. At the same time, the racquet must move across the back of the ball to generate spin. The strings are quite slippery, more so than the court. When the strings first contact the ball, they start slid-ing across the back of the ball, but then they grip the ball. The sliding and grip-ping actions drag the back of the ball in the same direction as the strings are moving, so the ball will spin in that direction.

Figure 4.4 shows views looking at the back of the ball, and the arrows indicate the direction of motion of the racquet as well as the position where the strings grip hold of the ball. The strings can drag along a line through the center of the ball (the three drawings on the left) or they can drag along a line off-center (the three drawings on the right). If the racquet head is rising upward as it strikes the ball, and if the racquet contacts the back of the ball along the center line, then the only spin that is generated is topspin. If the racquet head is moving downward when it strikes the ball, then the resulting spin is backspin. That action is not shown in Figure 4.4 because it is the same as topspin, but with the arrow pointing the other way. In fact each of the six arrows in Figure 4.4 can be reversed, which makes at least 12 different ways to hit a ball. Furthermore, the off-center arrows on the left side or the top side of the ball could equally well be drawn on the right side or the bottom side of the ball. That makes at least 18 different ways to hit the ball. There are even more ways if the bottom two drawings have the arrows sloping upward at different angles.

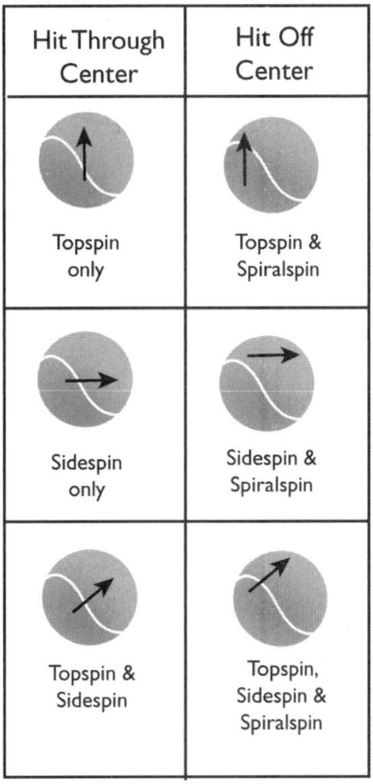

Hit Through Center	Hit Off Center
Topspin only	Topspin & Spiralspin
Sidespin only	Sidespin & Spiralspin
Topspin & Sidespin	Topspin, Sidespin & Spiralspin

Figure 4.4 *Six main ways to generate spin.*

Spin Before and After Bounce

The effect of the court or the strings on a spinning ball can be seen most easily by dropping a spinning ball vertically, as shown in Figure 4.5. If the ball has sidespin, then the spin axis is vertical. When a ball with sidespin hits the court, the bottom of the ball spins around on the court, and the rotation speed slows down because of friction between the ball and the court. But the friction does not act in any one direction, so the ball then bounces vertically up off the court, still spinning about its vertical axis, but with less spin than before. However, if the ball is spinning about one of the horizontal axes when it hits the court, then the ball bounces upwards and sideways. The direction of the sideways deflection is the direction in which the top of the ball is spinning. That's because the bottom of the ball slides backwards on the court, so the court acts by pushing the ball forward. It's like a sprinter pushing back on the blocks to accelerate forward.

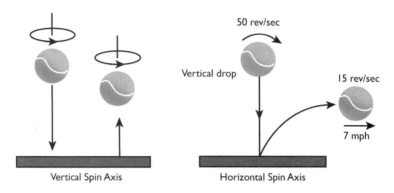

Figure 4.5 *The topspin or spiralspin ball "kicks" in the direction of spin at the top of the ball. The sidespin ball does not kick because it does not generate friction in any one direction. These effects occur both off the court and off the strings of a racquet. A spinning ball can therefore bounce at unexpected angles off each.*

The sideways kick of the ball is easy to explain. The hard part is to figure out how fast it kicks sideways and how fast the ball spins after it bounces. Both of these questions are fundamental in understanding how friction works in generating or in changing the spin of a ball, especially because the ball is usually spinning before it hits the court or the strings of a racquet.

Measurements of the sideways kick show that if the ball is spinning at 50 revolutions/second (3,000 rpm) about the horizontal axis just before it hits the court, and if the ball is dropped vertically, then it bounces sideways at a speed of about 7 mph and spinning at about 15 revolutions/second (900 rpm), regardless of whether the court is smooth or rough. The smoothness or roughness makes a small difference, but only a few percent. If the ball is spinning at 100 revolutions/second (6,000 rpm) just before it hits the court, then the ball bounces sideways at 14 mph spinning at 30 revolutions/second (1,800 rpm). Doubling the initial spin therefore doubles the sideways speed and spin, not because there is more friction, but because friction acts twice as long before the ball bites. However, above 100 revolutions/second the sideways speed and spin *does* depend on the roughness of the court because the ball then bounces before it stops its sliding motion. But spin rates above 100 revolutions/second are rarely ever seen in tennis.

EFFECT OF GRIP ON SPIN

One might expect that the friction force should be bigger on a rough surface, so a spinning ball dropped vertically should spin more slowly after it bounces.

The friction force is indeed bigger on a rough surface, but for normal rates of spin, the end result is the same on both smooth and rough surfaces, and it is the same if the ball bounces off smooth or rough tennis strings. The reason is that the spinning ball keeps sliding on the surface until it grips the surface, and from then on there is no further change in speed or spin (see Figure 4.6). On a rough surface it grips sooner.

Grip occurs when the bottom of the ball is no longer sliding on the surface. It doesn't mean that the whole ball comes to a stop. It means that if the ball starts rolling on the surface in such a way that the whole ball is moving forward at 14 mph, and the whole ball is spinning at 30 revolutions/second, then all points on the circumference of the ball are rotating at 14 mph (Figure 4.6a). As a result, when a point on the circumference rotates to the bottom of the ball,

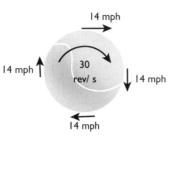

(a) Ball spinning at 30 rev/s about an axis at rest. All points on the circumference rotate at 14 mph relative to the middle of the ball.

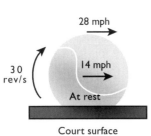

(b) Bottom of ball is at rest and grips the court but the whole ball is travelling to the right at 14 mph.

(c) The strings grip the left side of the ball because each is moving up at 20 mph. The whole ball is rising at only 6 mph since all points on the circumference rotate at 14 mph relative to the middle of the ball.

Figure 4.6 *When a ball first contacts a surface, it slides and rotates. When the contact area of the ball is moving at the same speed as the contact surface, the ball grips the surface. The ball spin then remains essentially constant until the ball bounces.*

then that point comes to rest on the surface, because it is spinning backward at 14 mph while the ball is moving forward at 14 mph (Figure 4.6b). When a ball starts rolling on a surface in this manner, the friction force drops to zero because there is no sliding of one surface past another. On a smooth surface the ball takes longer to start rolling, but when it does, it spins at the same rate as it does on a rough surface.

Rolling is just an instantaneous transition between sliding and biting. When the ball bites, not only has the ball come to rest relative to the surface, it also becomes stuck to the surface. In the case of a racquet, that means that the bottom of the ball moves with the racquet as in Figure 4.6c. This happens when the contact part of the ball is moving at the same speed as the strings. At that point the strings "grip" the ball, and the contact point between ball and strings does not change. To the courtside observer, the contact region of the ball and racquet are traveling the same speed and direction. If that is true, the two points stay in contact, as if stuck to each other, for the rest of the impact duration. In a sense, the courtside observer sees the ball and racquet glued together and spinning around as one object. Relative to the racquet, the backside of the ball is at rest. That is why sliding friction comes to a stop at this point and ceases to generate spin. So contrary to intuition and common discourse, it is when the strings grip the ball that the increase in spin stops, not when it starts. (See Match Point Box 4.2 for a discussion of whether players can feel the strings grip the ball.)

Can Racquets and Strings Increase Spin?

How do you create more friction and make it last as long as possible in order to generate more spin? Common tennis lore says that you can use:

  Tighter strings/looser strings
  Denser string pattern/open string pattern
  Thinner strings
  Rougher strings
  Soft strings like natural gut
  Polyurethane coated strings

The belief is that altering these variables will create more friction for the purpose of grabbing the ball and then rotating it into as much spin as possible.

Each of the methods above does indeed affect *how* friction acts, but not the end result of that action. That fact is that all strings achieve about the same results with respect to spin. Some combinations of strings, patterns, and tensions do

Match Point Box 4.2

Can Players Feel Spin?

An interesting question is whether players can feel the strings grabbing the ball. Perhaps certain combinations of string material, tension, gauge, pattern, coating, etc., that cause higher friction forces for shorter time create a perceptible impulse to the hand, whereas combinations that create lower forces for a longer time may generate impulses below some perceptual threshold. It is somewhat analogous to catching a baseball in a short time with a big force by holding your glove still, or catching it over a longer time with a smaller force by moving your hand backward as the ball settles into the glove. The strings grabbing the ball is like the hand catching the baseball. You can feel one set of conditions more than the other. If players can indeed feel the difference, perhaps it is with the combinations of equipment that maximize this impulse that they say has the best spin potential.

If the equipment is configured to create high impact forces (e.g., high tension) and have a high coefficient of friction (roughness), then the force of the ball parallel to the strings will be greater, and the friction force resisting this will also be more. A player may be able to feel a greater force pushing the racquet in a direction parallel to the strings, and, also, may be able to feel the quick diminishment of the force in the same direction. In other words, it is possible there is a catching sensation. However, as the text points out, whether you can feel friction at work or not, the spin rate will be the same, no matter the stringbed configuration.

it by achieving a higher friction force over a smaller time and others by a lower force over a longer time. But laboratory experiments show that the end result is always the same spin.

You can increase spin by changing the racquet path or speed or by tilting your racquet, but not by altering the stringbed. Different shots alter spin by varying the racquet path, speed, or tilt in order to affect the magnitude, duration, and direction of friction. For any given shot, altering the stringbed will not make a difference in the spin.

So spin depends only on the speed of the racquet head in a direction parallel to the string plane (or the equivalent actions of swinging at a steeper angle or tilting the racquet). That's so because it then takes friction longer to bring the ball to bite, during which time more spin is generated. You don't get more spin from the strings, only from stroke technique. Your equipment may cause you to hit your stroke differently, and that may cause more spin. But the equipment itself has very little, if any, direct affect on spin.

INCREASING SPIN WITH STROKE TECHNIQUE

In order to increase the spin off the strings, you can do three things. First, you can hit the ball harder. Suppose the racquet head slides across the back of the ball at 10 mph. The ball will start to rotate if it wasn't already spinning, and it will continue to rotate faster until the back of the ball is also traveling at 10 mph. At that point sliding stops and the strings grip the ball. The ball can't rotate any faster after that because it sticks to the strings until it bounces off them. The back of the ball comes off the strings spinning 10 mph faster than the middle of the ball, in a direction at right angles to the path of the ball. The ball will then be spinning at 22 revolutions/second, or 1,320 rpm. To increase the spin, the racquet needs to travel faster than 10 mph across the back of the ball. At 20 mph the ball will spin at 44 revolutions/second. At 40 mph the spin will be 88 revolutions/second.

Second, you can make the racquet rise up faster by bringing the racquet up at a steeper angle. The extreme case of that is a topspin lob. Bringing the racquet up at a steeper angle makes the ball spin faster, and it also makes the ball go higher over the net.

The third thing is to tilt the racquet head forward so the strings are no longer in a vertical plane. That is equivalent to having the ball approach the strings at an angle farther from a right angle path. It will also have the effect of hitting the ball downward. If you hit the ball from waist height with this technique, then the ball might go into the net. To compensate, the racquet head has to rise upward at a steeper angle, or faster.

Tilting the racquet head forward slightly helps to generate spin when you are returning the ball around shoulder height. There are two reasons. First, it is difficult to swing the racquet head upward at a steep angle when you are already reaching up high to start your swing. Second, you need to hit the ball down over the net rather than up over the net.

Tilting the racquet head is much easier with the wider oversize racquets of today compared to years ago. Players used topspin and backspin in the old days, but the amount of spin was limited by the fact that the racquet head needed to remain vertical as they swung the racquet head upward for topspin or downward for backspin. That way the area of the string plane that was seen by the ball was large enough for the ball to hit the strings and bounce off without touching the frame on the way in or on the way out. By keeping the head vertical, the sliding distance of the ball across the strings was kept to a minimum, which also helped to keep the ball away from the edge of the frame. With the advent of wider, oversize racquets, players could tilt the racquet and still present as much string area to the ball as they could while keeping the racquet face vertical with the narrower wood frames years ago. An extra inch in head width also allows for an extra inch of sliding, which can easily increase the amount of topspin by a factor of four or more when the ball is incident with backspin (as shown in Figure 4.10). Figure 4.7 shows how the larger frame makes tilting the frame a viable option for creating spin. It also shows (if you think about it) that a 10-inch racquet can be swung upwards at 26 degrees to the horizontal, and it will present the same string area to the ball as a 9-inch racquet swung horizontally.

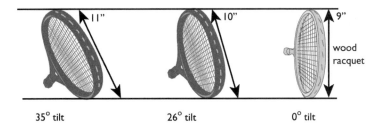

35° tilt   26° tilt   0° tilt

Figure 4.7 *A 10-inch wide racquet can be tilted by 26 degrees and it will present the same string area to the ball as an old wood racquet. An 11-inch racquet can be tilted at 35 degrees to present the same area. In fact, most professional players use a 10-inch-wide racquet because there is no need to tilt the racquet head as far as 35 degrees and because a smaller head is more maneuverable.*

SIMPLE TOPSPIN EXPERIMENT

It is difficult to generate much topspin in a serve by swinging the racquet upward as it contacts the ball. The problem is that the racquet is almost as high as it can go when it contacts the ball. So how do players manage to hit a serve with topspin? Allowing the ball to fall onto the strings with a high ball toss helps a bit, but it can't be the whole story because the ball falls too slowly. A better technique is to tilt the racquet head forward when it strikes the ball. Even if a player strikes the ball when the string plane is vertical, the racquet head will have tilted forward by the time the ball leaves the strings. The ball

Match Point Box 4.3

Topspin and the Federer Forehand

Roger Federer is one of those rare players who doesn't seem to have a weakness in his game. Not only that, he can hit a winner from any part of the court from seemingly impossible positions at seemingly impossible angles. Just how he does it is hard to say, which is why people like John Yandell from Advanced Tennis (www.tennisplayer.net) have been capturing his and other top players' shots on high speed video film for further analysis. A whole book could be written on this topic, but we have room to show only two such shots, a Federer forehand hit from the baseline and a Sampras serve (see "The Sampras Serve"), each captured on film at 125 frames/second.

In the forehand shot (Figure 4.8), the racquet was arched over the head into a ready position well behind the back and then accelerated rapidly toward the ball in an upward sweeping arc. The ball was struck well in front of the body, just above waist height, with the racquet head tilted forward about 8 degrees and rising upward at 31 degrees at impact. The drawing marks the position of the ball and the tip of the racquet at intervals of $1/125 = 0.008$ seconds. From that information we found that the speed of the racquet tip was 81 mph at impact and the outgoing speed of the ball was 96 mph.

It is clear from these measurements that the outgoing ball speed depends mainly on the speed of the racquet head. The bounce off the strings also contributes to the outgoing ball speed. If the ball was approaching a stationary racquet at 29 mph, it would bounce off the strings at about $0.4 \times 29 = 12$ mph. If the impact point on the racquet head is traveling at 70 mph (the tip travels a bit faster) and strikes a stationary ball, then the outgoing ball speed will be about $1.4 \times 70 = 98$ mph. However, Roger's racquet was traveling upward at 31 degrees to the horizontal and had a forward speed of only about 60 mph. So the expected forward speed of the ball is about $1.4 \times 60 = 84$ mph if the ball is initially at rest. Adding a rebound speed of 12 mph, since the ball was approaching at 29 mph, gives a predicted outgoing ball speed of $84 + 12 = 96$ mph, exactly as measured. Using a different string or a different string tension or a heavier or lighter racquet might change that result by one or two miles per hour, but the main factor determining the outgoing ball speed is the forward speed of the racquet head before impact. The outgoing ball speed would have been faster if the racquet head was traveling horizontally at impact, but the ball would then have been hit with almost zero topspin.

Others have also taken high-speed video, sometimes with two cameras simultaneously to get a full three-dimensional view of events. People who study biomechanics and many tennis coaches use video film in

Match Point Box 4.3 continued

this manner to determine the motion of each part of the body and to determine whether players have any particular faults in stroke style. In almost every case, interest is focused on motion of the legs, torso, upper arm, and forearm. The collision of the racquet and the ball rarely gets a mention. Consequently, there is still a lot to learn about this subject. For example, many coaches still believe that the racquet face must be vertical to hit a topspin forehand or backhand. However, Roger Federer and many other players tilt the racquet head forward, especially on shots hit above the waist. Sometimes, the ball is struck not in the middle of the strings but lower down near the frame. As a result, the racquet head rotates during the shot so that the head is tilted forward by the time the ball leaves the strings.

From the speed of the racquet head and its tilt, one can estimate the spin of the ball as it comes off the strings. For the Federer forehand, the ball is spinning at around 95 revolutions/second, which means that it rotates about 60 times through the air as it travels from one end of the court to the other.

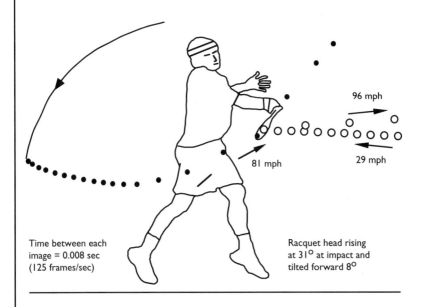

96 mph

81 mph

29 mph

Time between each
image = 0.008 sec
(125 frames/sec)

Racquet head rising
at 31° at impact and
tilted forward 8°

Figure 4.8 *The Federer Forehand*

remains on the strings while the racquet swings forward about 8 to 12 inches, depending on racquet head speed.

The effect of tilting the racquet head can be seen by a simple experiment. Take a ruler and a coin and put them flat on a table. Bring the ruler up to the coin as shown in Figure 4.9a and keep pushing the ruler slowly forward (to the left) and upward. That simulates the action in a topspin forehand where the racquet head rises as it moves forward. The coin will rotate slowly with topspin. If you hit the coin with the ruler, by pushing the ruler faster, then the coin will slide to a stop along the table and you will see that the coin has rotated. The amount of spin and upward thrust given to the coin depends on friction between the coin and the ruler. If the edges of the coin and the ruler are both fairly smooth the coin will move forward without much upward motion and without much spin. It's the same with a ball and tennis strings, but the strings always get a good grip on the ball because the ball squashes onto the strings. The coin touches the ruler at only one point. If you glue a rubber band around the edge of the coin it will behave more like a tennis ball because the ruler will get a better grip. Or you could use a bottle top or cork, or roughen the edge with a file.

Now tilt the ruler forward as shown in Figure 4.9b and push it forward without pushing it upward. The coin rolls down the ruler with topspin. The two effects shown in Figures 4.9a and 4.9b are exactly the same. That's because Figure 4.9b is exactly the same as Figure 4.9a except it has been rotated on the page. If you don't believe it, then rotate the page. Tilting the racquet head forward and swinging it horizontally therefore has almost exactly the same effect as a low to high swing while the strings remain vertical. The only difference is

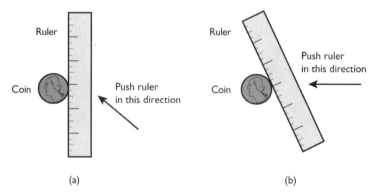

(a)   (b)

Figure 4.9 *A simple experiment to show that tilting the racquet face creates topspin just as does hitting up into the ball at an angle.*

that the ball is projected downward when the racquet head is tilted and is projected upward in a low to high swing. Figure 4.9a therefore represents a topspin forehand or backhand, and Figure 4.9b represents a topspin serve.

The easiest way to hit a topspin serve this way is to toss the ball forward and strike the ball *after* the racquet has reached its highest point. Players who toss the ball slightly behind their head and arch their back to serve can also hit a topspin serve by tilting the racquet forward with their wrist so the racquet tip swings ahead of the handle. A racquet works in the same way that a golf club works. Just as clubs are tilted backward to impart backspin, racquets can also be tilted backward to impart backspin or forward for topspin.

EFFECT OF RACQUET TILT ON A TOPSPIN FOREHAND

When graphite replaced wood in the late 1970s, players and coaches discovered that the lighter frames and the larger head allowed players to swing at the ball in different ways. Players were able to swing the racquet faster, upward at a steeper angle, and across the flight of the ball to generate more topspin and more sidespin, and they could use wrist action to generate even greater racquet head speed. In the old days, players swung the racquet more or less in line with the flight path, continued to swing in that direction with the follow through, and locked their wrist to stop the heavy racquet head falling behind. It took modern players a bit longer to discover that they could generate even more spin by tilting the racquet head forward by changing to a Western or extreme Western grip. Because that grip is useless for a backhand, players had to change to a double-handed backhand grip to tilt the racquet head forward.

The effect of tilting the racquet head is shown in Figure 4.10. It was assumed that the ball approaches the player along a horizontal path at 33 mph and is spinning at 3,820 rpm with topspin. A spin of 3,820 rpm is a typical ball spin generated when the ball bounces off the court. The racquet head is swung toward the ball at 45 mph. Figure 4.10 shows the result of swinging the racquet in four different ways. These are calculated rather than measured results, but they are based on measurements of the bounce off a hand-held racquet. Note how the ball kicks upwards off the strings in (Figure 4.10a), even though the ball is incident at right angles to the strings. This is caused by the effect shown in Figure 4.5. In order to stop the ball kicking up like this, it is necessary to tilt the racquet head forward (Figure 4.10c) or to swing the racquet slightly downwards. Another solution is to swing upwards so that the ball comes off the strings with topspin (Figure 4.10b). It will then dive down onto the court after it passes over the net, despite the upward kick off the strings.

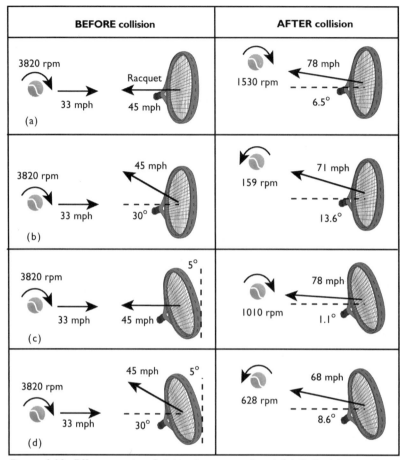

Figure 4.10 *Effect on spin of tilting the racquet head. (a) Ball with topspin and racquet approach along same path. (b) Racquet swung upward into ball. (c) Ball and racquet approach on same horizontal path, but racquet is tilted forward 5 degrees. (d) Racquet approaches ball both with an upward path and a forward tilt.*

If the racquet head is vertical and approaches the ball along the same horizontal path as the ball, then the ball will be deflected upward at an angle of 6.5 degrees above the horizontal, and it will come off the strings at a speed of 78 mph and spinning at 1,530 rpm. However, the ball is returned with backspin. The direction of spin is not reversed in this case, so the ball spins clockwise before it hits the strings and also spins clockwise after it bounces.

Figure 4.10b shows the effect of swinging the racquet head upward at an angle of 30 degrees to the horizontal. The ball comes off the strings at a higher angle, at reduced speed and with only a small amount of topspin (159 rpm). In order to generate more topspin, a player would need to swing the racquet faster or tilt the racquet head forward, or both.

Figure 4.10c shows the result of tilting the racquet head forward by 5 degrees but swinging along the same horizontal path as the incoming ball. The result is a low trajectory and a reduced amount of backspin compared with Figure 4.10a. Five degrees of tilt by itself is not enough to generate topspin. However, if the racquet head is rising at 30 degrees and is also tilted forward by five degrees (Figure 4.10d), then there is a big increase in the amount of topspin compared with Figure 4.10b. The trajectory is also five degrees lower. Most of the work is done by swinging the racquet upward, which changes the spin from -3,820 rpm to +159 rpm. Tilting the racquet five degrees changes the paltry 159 rpm into a more respectable 628 rpm of topspin. The extra topspin is due to the smaller angle of incidence, which allows the friction force to act for a longer time before the strings grip the ball. The strings also slide for a greater distance across the ball before they grip (or vice-versa), which was not easy to do without clipping the frame when using old wood racquets.

More topspin could be generated by tilting the racquet head further forward, but the trajectory would then be too low, unless the racquet is swung up at angle greater than 30 degrees or the ball is hit from around shoulder height.

SPIN AND THE SERVE

BALL TOSS

How high should you toss the ball, and when should you hit it? Different coaches have different opinions about this because there is no best answer. Watch the professionals and you will see lots of different tosses. Some throw it really high and wait for a second or more for it to fall into the hitting zone. Others have a really low toss and seem to hit it on the way up only a split second after they have released it. Another thing to notice is that every player has a different serve action, especially in the preparation stage. Some players bounce the ball six times before they are ready to serve, others step straight up and whack it. There is no best technique here either, but it is important to develop a consistent rhythm. If you do something different every time you serve, then you will end up with a different result.

From a physics point of view there are several different effects. One is that hitting the ball at the top of the toss allows you to hit the ball while it is almost completely stopped. That way you won't have any significant timing or positioning problem. You can hit the ball just before or just after the ball reaches its maximum height, and the ball will move up or down less than a few millimeters. In fact, the ball remains within half an inch (12.7 millimeters) of its highest point for 0.1 seconds. During that time your racquet will swing forward about six feet. Hence, you can hit the ball at almost the same point on the strings every time, provided you toss the ball to the same height every time. However, if you throw the ball too far forward, you will hit it into the bottom of the net. Too far back, and the ball will tend to land near the baseline.

Hitting the ball on the way down, after a high ball toss, gives you extra time to make fine adjustments to your serve action. In fact, the ball will take 0.43 seconds to drop three feet from its highest point. You might toss the ball too far forward or backward, but at least you will have enough time to see where the ball is going and to adjust your swing accordingly. Pat Rafter often had trouble with that and would let the ball drop to the court and say, "Sorry, mate." What he was really thinking was that he would toss the next ball just as high because that way he could get extra topspin on the ball. A few years ago in Sydney, Australia, a player did the same thing and uttered a loud "Sorry." Six thousand spectators instantly added "mate" because that's what they were used to hearing.

In order to hit a ball with topspin, the racquet head needs to rise up to meet the ball and to keep moving up during the shot. If you hit the ball at the top of the swing or on the way down, then you can't impart any topspin unless you tilt the racquet head forward. An alternative is to use a bit of Einstein's relativity to get around the problem. Topspin is generated whenever the racquet head is rising *or* when the ball is falling. The higher you toss the ball, the faster it will fall, and the more topspin you will get. Sampras used to toss the ball up 12 feet and let it fall almost two feet before hitting it.

TIPS ON SERVING

When people first started playing lawn tennis in England in the 1850s, they served underarm to get the point started. It was soon discovered that players could do better serving overarm, and it has been that way ever since. In fact, the serve is now a common way of finishing the point, if not by an ace or unplayable serve, then by a double fault. The temptation is to hit the first serve as fast as possible in an attempt to win the point and to hit the second serve as slowly as possible to make sure it goes in. That strategy rarely works. Instead, you need to optimize your chances by getting around 70 percent of first serves in and around 95 percent of second serves in. To do that you need to realize that the faster you serve, the less likely you are to get the serve in.

There is only a small range of serve angles above or below the horizontal that will allow the ball to pass over the net and land in the service box. If the ball is served as fast as possible in a horizontal direction, then it will hit the back fence. If the ball is served 10 degrees below the horizontal, then it will land in the bottom of the net. In order for a flat, fast serve to be good, the ball needs to be hit about five or six degrees below the horizontal. The range of good angles is only about two degrees for a fast serve or about four degrees for a medium pace second serve.

Everyone has trouble with his first serve because it is difficult to get the angle right, especially if you toss the ball too far forward or back. If you can get the angle right to within one degree, then you are doing well. However if it is sometimes one degree too high or too low, then about half your fast serves will be a fault. To improve on that you need to be more consistent with your ball toss and serve action, and/or you need to slow the serve.

There are three other factors that affect your chances of getting a serve in. They are the impact point on the racquet, the amount of topspin, and whether you serve over the high or the low part of the net.

Tall players can serve faster than short players because they see more of the service box. There is therefore a bigger range of angles in which to hit a good serve. You can make yourself effectively four inches taller by serving from a point near the tip of the racquet instead of from the middle of the strings. The tip travels faster than the middle, but the tip is also the least powerful part of the racquet. As a result, serve speed off the tip is slightly lower, but the combination of extra height and lower ball speed allow you to get more serves in.

A ball hit with topspin also gives a larger range of good serve angles. The ball still needs to be hit downward a few degrees below the horizontal, but not as far down as a flat serve. Players using topspin get the feeling they are hitting the ball upward because the racquet travels up to meet the ball, but the ball drops down from the high toss and bounces down below the horizontal as it comes off the strings.

You can serve over the low part of the net toward the tee, or you can serve wide over the high part of the net. Which is better in terms of the angles? It turns out that the range of good serve angles is almost exactly the same because the service court is shorter straight down the middle than diagonally across to the far corner. However, the range of good serve angles drops rapidly if you try to serve any wider than the far corner. In that case you can afford to slow the serve down because the ball will be hard to return even at medium pace, especially if you spin the ball so that it kicks out sideways away from the receiver.

ARCHING THE BACK TO SERVE

Why do some top players arch backward when they serve? It's not strictly necessary, and it puts extra strain on the back, so why do they do it? It looks as if they tossed the ball too far to the left so they need to bend over backward to reach it. In addition, there is usually a big bend in the knees, so the player can arch even further backward and spring back up as the racquet swings up and forward. The answer is that it helps to get more spin on the ball.

When hitting a topspin forehand or backhand, the strings remain in a vertical plane (or close to it) while the racquet head rises up to meet the ball and continues upward through the stroke. That way, the strings grab the back of the ball and rotate it in a direction from the bottom of the ball to the top. If you imagine a clock face on the back of the ball with 12 o'clock on top, then the ball rotates from 6 to 12 o'clock. That's almost impossible to do when serving because the racquet head can't rise much farther when it is already near the top of its swing. In addition, the strings can't remain in a vertical plane if you swing the racquet from a point behind your back to a point in front of your body. In that case, hitting the ball while the racquet head is rising will send the ball up into the sky (Figure 4.11).

If you toss the ball straight up in front of you and swing your racquet overhead and straight toward the intended landing point, then you can serve the ball fast, but with very little spin. That type of serve is called a "flat" serve, and the racquet finishes up on your left side after the follow through. If you toss the ball farther to the left and repeat the same basic action (assuming you are right-handed), then the ball will land farther to the left. Alternatively, as shown in Figure 4.12, if you arch backwards, you can swing the racquet up and across the back of the ball from about the 8 o'clock to about the 2 o'clock position. The racquet ends up on your right side after striking the ball. That way, the racquet is still moving upward when it contacts the ball because it is moving in an arc that is rising from left to right (as well as in an arc from behind your back and toward the net).

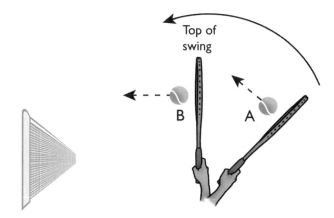

Flat serve viewed side-on

Figure 4.11 *In an attempt to hit topspin, you can't hit up into the ball and straight on without sending the ball into the sky.*

Arched back serve viewed from behind

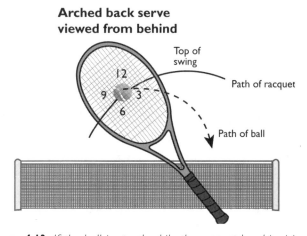

Figure 4.12 *If the ball is struck while the racquet head is rising from 8 to 2 o'clock then the ball will have topspin and sidespin.*

The racquet reaches the top of its left to right arc in front of your right shoulder, so if you hit the ball above your left shoulder the racquet head is still rising upward. The ball needs to be tossed more to the left and farther back than usual. The left-to-right motion allows you to keep the strings in an almost vertical plane, as in a topspin backhand. You also need to swing the racquet forward so the ball goes over the net, which means that the strings don't remain exactly in a vertical plane.

The ball acquires topspin, but it also acquires some sidespin. In other words, if the ball is actually rotating from 8 to 2 o'clock, then that is equivalent to rotation from 6 to 12 o'clock *plus* rotation from 9 to 3 o'clock. The topspin part causes the ball to dive down onto the court, and the sidespin part causes the ball to curve to the left as the ball heads over the net. The penalty is that the serve speed is lower, but the advantage is that the serve is more likely to go in.

SLICE SERVE

In order to serve a ball with topspin, you need to toss the ball to the left if you are right-handed. To serve a slice serve, you need to toss the ball to your right. That way you need to reach out and hit the right side of the ball to hit it into play. The strings should hit the back of the ball and then continue toward the 3 o'clock position so that the ball spins around a vertical axis from left to right as you face it. There is no need to arch backwards for a slice serve, but you need to turn and face along the baseline rather than facing the net, at least when starting to serve.

SERVE ACTIONS

Of all the various tennis shots, the serve is the most important, and it is also the most complicated. Every body segment rotates and twists and turns in such a strange sequence that it is very difficult to describe in any sort of logical way. Even if we forget about the legs, torso, and arms and just concentrate on what the racquet is doing, the result is pretty amazing.

All that the racquet really needs to do is swing forward in a smooth arc, accelerating on the way, until it collides with the ball. Instead, the racquet usually starts from a point in front of the player, moves down past the ankles, then up behind the shoulder, back down again before climbing way up over the head. After striking the ball, the racquet swings down to the knee and back across the front of the body. While the racquet is following this tortuous path, the wrist is busy twisting it around. Just before impact, the racquet rises up rapidly behind the shoulder with the strings in a vertical plane, as if the player is about to chop the ball in half with the edge of the racquet. Instead, the player rotates the wrist at the last second so that the ball will be struck by the full face of the strings. While that is going on, the elbow is rotating the racquet both upward and forward. If the player wants to spin the ball, then the racquet also needs to move across the back of the ball. It might appear that the wrist is used to wrap the racquet around to one side of the ball, but the ball has usually left the strings by that time.

To catch all the action, it is necessary to film it with a high-speed camera. Match Point Box 4.4 shows several views of a Pete Sampras serve captured by John Yandell (www.tennisplayer.net) at 125 frames per second (Figures 4.13 and 4.14). The most interesting view, in terms of the actual impact of the racquet with the ball, is the view from above (Figure 4.14). It shows the racquet head twisting around and moving across the back of the ball as it swings forward. Almost all players twist the racquet around in this manner, using the wrist. If they didn't, the ball would be struck by the front edge of the frame rather than the strings. The only alternative is to start off with a different grip, with the racquet in front of the body and the strings in a horizontal plane. It's the way young children serve the ball when they first learn to play. The racquet is lifted straight up over the shoulder and then swings forward in a simple up and down arc with no wrist rotation at all.

The racquet makes contact with the ball when the racquet is pointing toward its intended destination. The ball therefore heads off in the correct direction, even though the head continues to rotate about a vertical axis after the impact. While the head moves forward, it also moves across the back of the ball, causing it to spin about a vertical axis. Served to the forehand court and into the far corner, the ball will swerve in the air away from the receiver, forcing him out wide.

FOREARM SLOWS DOWN

Apart from the fact that Sampras hit the ball at the very top of the swing, two features of the serve action pictured in Match Point Box 4.4 deserve special mention because they are unexpected. The first is that the forearm slows down just before impact. One might expect that the forearm should accelerate to maximum speed at impact. In fact, it has been found with tennis players, golfers, and baseball players that the forearm always slows down just before impact. The reason is that it is the swing speed of the racquet (or the club or the bat) that needs to be a maximum at impact, not the forearm. The slowing down of the forearm is not a deliberate action by the player. It is caused by the backward force of the handle on the player's hand. If the racquet head rotates forward rapidly, then the handle tends to rotate backward, or at least slow down in the forward direction. The backward torque on the handle then acts to rotate the head forward even faster.

The interaction between the racquet and the forearm can be modeled as a double pendulum, that is, one pendulum attached to the end of another (see Figure 1.13). If one films a double pendulum, it is easy to see that the upper

Match Point Box 4.4

The Sampras Serve

Sampras had such a good, consistent serve that he often hit his second serve faster than most people hit a first serve. The serve shown in Figure 4.13 is typical of the style used by many other players in that there is usually a long windup phase with the racquet head dropping down behind the back before it accelerates to maximum speed at impact. The end result is that the ball comes off the strings at a speed only slightly higher than the speed of the racquet tip. In other words, the serve speed depends almost entirely on the speed at which the player swings the racquet, regardless of the type of string,

string tension, or weight of the racquet, etc. These other factors can change the serve speed by a few mph, but 95 percent of serve speed is determined by the player, and only five percent is influenced by changing the racquet and the strings.

Given that the tip was traveling at 94 mph, we can estimate that a point four inches down from the tip was traveling at about 80 mph. In the middle of the strings, the rebound power (ACOR) is typically about 0.4, but 4 inches from the tip it is about 0.3 for a moderately heavy racquet. Without knowing anything else about the particular

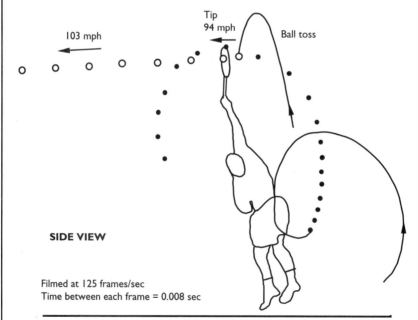

Figure 4.13 *Side view of the serve motion of Pete Sampras.*

Match Point Box 4.4 continued

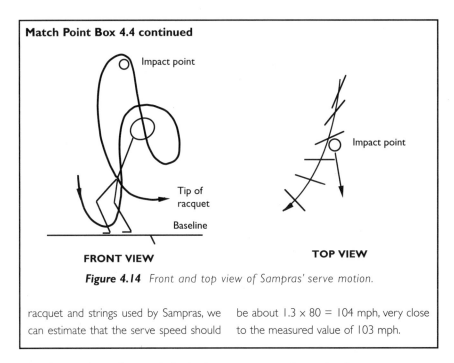

FRONT VIEW   **TOP VIEW**

Figure 4.14 *Front and top view of Sampras' serve motion.*

racquet and strings used by Sampras, we can estimate that the serve speed should be about $1.3 \times 80 = 104$ mph, very close to the measured value of 103 mph.

arm always slows down while the lower arm speeds up. In that way, rotational energy gained by the upper arm is transferred to the lower arm. Similar effects are observed in all throwing and kicking activities. That is, the upper arm or the upper leg slows down while the forearm or lower leg speeds up. When swinging a racquet, bat, or club, the forearm needs to slow down to transfer its energy to the implement in the hand.

FORCE ON HANDLE

The second unexpected result concerns the force exerted on the handle. In order to get the racquet up to speed, starting from a position where the racquet is behind the back, the player pulls up on the handle and then pushes it forward. Just before impact, the forces are in the exact opposite directions. That is, the player pulls backward on the handle (since the forearm and the hand are slowing down) and pulls downward. The downward pull is, in fact, very large, about equal to the weight of the player. It is necessary to pull downward so the racquet doesn't fly up into the sky, as it would if the player let go of the handle while the racquet was rising. The downward pull is known as a centripetal force, and it is proportional to the speed of the racquet squared. If Sampras was using a 360-gram racquet and swung the tip in an arc of radius 30 inches at a speed of 94 mph, then the downward force on the handle was about 170 pounds. In other words, Sampras could support his own weight just by pulling down on the handle, which helps to explain why most players lift off the court when serving. Actually, liftoff occurs while the player is pulling the racquet upward from behind the back, but the player can then remain airborne by pulling down on the handle.

TRAJECTORY

VERTICAL LAUNCH ANGLE

At what vertical angle should you hit the ball over the net? It depends on where you are standing, the type of shot, and what you are attempting to do, but some typical ball trajectories are shown in Figures 4.15 and 4.16 as a guide. Figure 4.15 shows that a 110 mph serve hit nine feet above the court surface must be served down from the horizontal to land in the service box, regardless of whether it is a flat or topspin serve. There is only a 1.4 degree range of good angles for a flat serve where the ball either just clears the net or lands on the service line. If the ball has 40 revolutions/second (2,400 rpm) of topspin, the range of good angles increases to 2.5 degrees. Given that it is hard to maintain an accuracy of one degree in the serve angle, a topspin serve is more likely to go in than a flat serve. Because a topspin serve hits the court at a steeper angle, it will also bounce up at a steeper angle.

Figure 4.16 shows four different trajectories for a groundstroke hit at 67 mph from a point about three feet above the baseline. The ball must be hit upward (rather than downward) to make it over the net, but not too high, otherwise it will land past the other baseline 78 feet away. The range of angles available for a good shot increases when topspin is used, and the ball bounces at a steeper angle when it lands on the court because it is incident at a steeper angle. It also bounces to a greater height because it hits the court at a greater vertical speed.

If you hit a ball horizontally from waist or net height, the ball will not go over the net. Gravity always pulls the ball down. Hit from waist height, a ball has to be hit at an angle above the horizontal in order to go over the net.

When serving a ball from a few feet above your head, if you hit the ball horizontally, it will land in the service box only if the serve is slow to medium pace. A fast serve hit horizontally will land somewhere near the baseline and possibly in the back fence. Fast serves must be hit at an angle below the horizontal, even when hit with topspin.

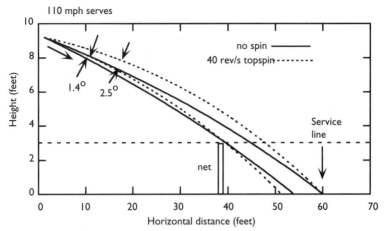

Figure 4.15 *Various trajectories for a good 110 mph serve, with and without topspin.*

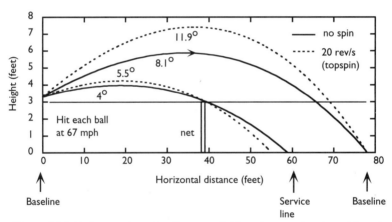

Figure 4.16 *Various trajectories for a good 67 mph groundstroke, with and without topspin.*

The ball trajectories shown in Figures 4.15 and 4.16 take into account the force of the air on the ball as well as the force of gravity. The force of the air is actually bigger than the force of gravity at the start of a fast serve. The biggest force of all is the force of the strings on the ball, but that force drops to zero as soon as the ball leaves the strings. If it wasn't for the air and gravity, a ball served at 110 mph would travel in a dead straight line at 110 mph until it hit something. Gravity acts to pull the ball down toward the court and, therefore, makes it travel in a curved path. The force of gravity on the ball is exactly equal to the weight of the ball, by definition, and it acts vertically downward. The force of gravity on a 57-gram (0.126 lb) ball is 0.126 pound (or 0.559 Newton in scientific units).

The ball cuts a path through the air by pushing it out of the way, which results in a backward force on the ball called the drag force. At 10 mph, the drag force on a tennis ball is only 0.00512 pounds, which is 24.6 times smaller than the weight of the ball. The drag force on a ball increases by four times when the ball speed doubles, and it increases 100 times when the ball speed increases by a factor of 10. At 100 mph, the drag is therefore 0.512 pounds, which is 4.1 times greater than the weight of the ball. As a result, a ball served at 110 mph hits the court at only 82 mph. The drag force is slightly larger if the ball becomes fuzzy, and it is slightly less at high altitudes since the air is thinner.

An additional force (the Magnus force) acts on the ball when it is spinning, and it acts vertically down when the ball has topspin, or vertically up when the ball has backspin. The Magnus force is typically about three times smaller than the drag force, which means it can also be larger than the force of gravity at the start of a fast serve. The Magnus force increases four times when the ball speed doubles, but it doesn't increase four times when the ball spin doubles. In fact, it increases by only about 45 percent when the ball spin doubles. In other words, if you can make the ball spin twice as fast, then the ball will curve more sharply through the air, but only slightly more, not twice as much.

HITTING THE BALL DEEP

All tennis players know that they should generally try to hit their return shot as deep as possible to make it difficult for their opponents to return the ball. The problem is that there is a 50-50 chance that the ball will be long if you aim to land right on the baseline. The solution is to aim a few feet short of the baseline. That way, most of your returns will be in, even if some of those returns land short. The problem is illustrated quite dramatically by the calculations shown in Figure 4.17. These calculations show what happens if you hit the ball too hard, too high, or without enough topspin.

As in Figure 4.16, we assumed that the ball was hit at a point one meter (3.28 feet) above the baseline, and it was hit either 8 or 10 degrees above the horizontal with topspin. The amount of topspin is shown along the bottom axis, and the distance traveled by the ball before it lands is shown along the vertical axis. Ideally, you want the ball to travel 78 feet to land on your opponent's

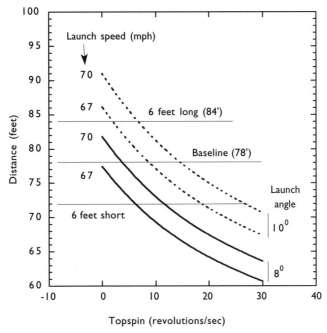

Figure 4.17 *Hitting a ball from one baseline to land on the other isn't easy. The two baselines are 78 feet apart. The four graphs show where the ball lands (vertical axis) vs amount of topspin (horizontal axis) when the ball is hit either at 67 mph or 70 mph and when the ball is hit at an angle of either 8 degrees (the solid curves) or 10 degrees (the dashed curves) above the horizontal. A ball hit with backspin at these speeds and angles would land at even greater distances.*

baseline (assuming you hit the ball along the court rather than across court). For example, if you hit the ball at 67 mph without any topspin, then you need to hit it 8.1 degrees above the horizontal to land on the far baseline (as shown in Figure 4.16). With 20 revolutions/second (1,200 rpm) of topspin, you would need to hit the ball 11.9 degrees above the horizontal to make it land on the far baseline.

The graph shows how easy it is to hit the ball six feet short or six feet long. If you hit the ball two degrees too high, it will land about nine feet beyond the baseline without topspin, or about seven feet beyond the baseline if you hit with 30 revolutions/second (1,800 rpm) of topspin. That means you need to get the launch angle right to better than one degree to land within four feet of the baseline. That's not impossible, but it requires lots of practice. Hit one degree higher, a ball will pass eight inches higher over the net when it is hit 39

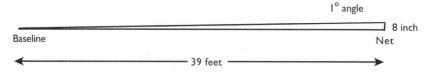

Figure 4.18 *Can you aim a ball within one degree? It takes practice, but that's what is needed to get a 70 mph return to land within four feet of the baseline. Slowing down the return (hitting a "moon ball" higher over the net) gives you a larger range of good angles and hence a better chance of success. Throwing a tennis ball into a one foot wide box or bucket 20 feet away also requires one degree accuracy. Is that any easier?*

feet away from the net (see Figure 4.18). Of course, you have to get the speed right too. Hitting the ball 3 mph too fast without topspin sends the ball 4.5 feet over the baseline or three feet beyond the baseline if you hit with 30 revolutions/second of topspin.

The moral of the story is that it is better to hit the ball with topspin, and you need lots of practice to get the angles and the speeds just right. If you still have trouble, then watch the professionals in action. They usually have trouble too, although some of them can strike a purple patch at times and get the ball to land within one foot of the baseline at least half the time. At other times they seem to have trouble getting the ball to land past the service line. They know how to do it, and can do it on the practice court, but tennis is a mind game as much as a game of skill. Physics can tell you what to do and why, and practice makes perfect, but if you have just lost the first set and your opponent is full of confidence, then it's time to rethink your game plan.

Further Reading

H. Brody, R. Cross and C. Lindsey, *The Physics and Technology of Tennis*, Racquet Tech Publishing, Solana Beach, USA (2002).

H. Brody, *Tennis Science for Tennis Players*, University of Pennsylvania Press, 1987.

R.D. Mehta and J.M. Pallis, The aerodynamics of a tennis ball, *Sports Engineering* 4, 177-189 (2001).

S.R. Goodwill and S.J. Haake, Ball spin generation for oblique impacts with a tennis racket, *Experimental Mechanics*, 44, 1-12 (2004).